CW00427787

A SCANDAL IN PLAIN SIGHT

Putting an end to a 60-year struggle and building an independent university in northwest Ireland

BY

GARRETT HARGAN

with contributions from Pat McArt,
the University of Edinburgh School of Architecture,
and the Derry University Group

Colmcille Press
Ráth Mór Centre
Derry, BT48 0LZ
info@colmcillepress.com
Managing Editor: Garbhan Downey

© 2024 in text Garrett Hargan, Pat McArt & others

Edited by Garrett Hargan

Layout/Design: Joe McAllister & Kevin Hippsley

The moral rights of the authors and contributors have been asserted in accordance with the Copyright, Designs and Patents Act, 1998.

Images courtesy individual contributors and Colmcille Press, Guildhall Press, Hive Studios, *Derry Journal, Derry News, Belfast Telegraph*.

First published July 2024

Colmcille Press gratefully acknowledges the support of Creggan Enterprises Limited and the John Bryson Foundation.

ISBN: 978-1-914009-43-3

A CIP copy for this book is available from the National Library of Ireland and the British Library.

All rights reserved. No part of this publication may be reproduced or transmitted in any form or by any means, electronic or mechanical, including photocopy, recording, or any information storage or retrieval system, without permission in writing from the publisher. The book is sold subject to the condition that it shall not, by way of trade or otherwise, be lent, re-sold or otherwise circulated without the publisher's prior consent in any form of binding or cover other than that in which it is published and without a similar condition including this condition being imposed on the subsequent purchaser.

ACKNOWLEDGEMENTS

I'd like to offer special thanks to my parents, Liam and Máire, and brothers Emmett and Fionntan for always supporting me; to my partner Michelle for her love and encouragement over the years; my beautiful daughters Muirinn and Ennagh who have given me untold joy and inspired me to think more deeply about a better life for the generations behind me.

I want to recognise the contributions of the Derry University Group whose efforts have kept the university flame alive, to esteemed former *Derry Journal* editor and author Pat McArt and to Edinburgh University for their unique perspective on the issue.

I would like to thank editors at the *Belfast Telegraph* and past editors at the *Derry News* for giving me the opportunity to write about a subject of such import for the people of Derry.

And finally everyone who has spoken to me for stories, including local politicians and campaigners, those who have taken an interest or shared my stories to a wider audience because without the readers there is no point in writing.

ABOUT THE AUTHOR

A former staff reporter with *the Derry News*, Garrett Hargan joined *the Belfast Telegraph* as its North West multimedia journalist in 2021. He previously studied at St Joseph's Boys' School and the North West Regional College in Derry and Queen's University Belfast.

'Centres like Limerick and Newcastle in England evidence the benefits which can accrue to a community in terms of promoting local pride and a sense of belonging, social engagement, increased consumer base, arts, culture and the sciences and employment. A thriving university can serve as an anchor for a city but this has been long denied to Derry/ Londonderry. There is a need for a fresh vision, political support and the establishment of a network of creative cooperation across the region of the Derry City and Strabane Council area in partnership with Donegal with the aim of providing an independent university for Derry/Londonderry. The old model has not worked and is curtailing economic, educational and social development. Replacing it will bring challenges. These will not be the first which the region, with its capacity for skills, knowledge and wisdom has faced and met successfully.'

Terry Wright
Derry News, November 2019

CONTENTS

FOREWORD
It wouldn't happen in North Korea

By Garbhán Downey, Derry University Group

Following the vote, the Committee was wound down. John Hume subsequently claimed that the decision not to build the new university in Derry was the immediate cause of the Northern Ireland civil-rights movement and ended any hope of a peaceful solution to sectarian divides in the state.

It was then – and is today – a scandal.

Sixty years after the outrageous sectarian blocking of its new university, which drove tens of thousands of its citizens to the streets, Derry is still prevented from having its own third-level institution.

Make no mistake, Stormont knew exactly what it was doing in the 1960s when it targeted this ancient city – a European scholastic centre for 1500 years – for generational failure. Just as Stormont knew what it was doing in the 2000s when it invested all its money centralising university provision in Belfast.

Today, more than eighty percent of the North's students are now embedded in our economically-booming 'capital'. It wouldn't happen in North Korea.

Derry University Group campaigners Garbhán Downey and Conal McFeely, with Mike Amesbury MP (left), and Labour's Angela Rayner, during a lobby visit to Westminster in 2019.

The minuscule Higher Education provision which Derry does have is controlled from outside the city. If a lecturer at Magee College wants to turn up the heat in the classroom, they have to ring the admin headquarters in Coleraine to get the thermostat turned up. Or as one academic quipped, it's got so bad that if Derry wants to bless itself, it has to ask Belfast to send down the holy water.

There is no regional autonomy at Magee, no decision-making, no regional integrity and no regional accountability; there is no North West voice in any of the big decisions and, crucially, no independent regional revenue.

Belfast officials even attempted to introduce an edict removing the title 'Magee' from the Derry campus – a landmark site for 160 years – without recourse to anyone in the city-region. It is autocracy run riot.

Over the decades, many politicians and university 'fixers' – most well-meaning and a few bluffers – have promised to put right the scandal. But they have all faced the same seemingly insurmountable problems:

- **Sectarianism**: Derry and the North West is a largely Catholic region, while government and the institutional structures were designed by, and for decades controlled by, the Protestant majority, and the resulting imbalances have never been corrected even as that majority has waned.

- **Centralisation of resources in the capital/the Belfast Agenda**: even after the Good Friday Agreement introduced power-sharing in the North, Derry's economy has continued to decline. Development strategies for the capital such as the Belfast Agenda envisage it becoming a 'nation city', a mindset reflected by the Northern Ireland Civil Service.

- **The economic deficit in border regions and the still-existing political border**: Derry and Donegal have consistently the highest levels of deprivation, joblessness, poor health and poor educational attainment on the island.

- **Failing infrastructure (including the higher education sector)**: the eastern seaboard of the Northern Ireland state has been financed, developed and grown to the almost complete exclusion of the western region.

- **University and state interdependence**: Ulster University was constituted by the state to service the state and is currently heavily in debt to the state, which in turn supports the Belfast Agenda and the status quo.

Derry University Group campaigners Kevin Hippsley and Conal McFeely erect the 'Wall of Protest' hoarding in Foyle Road in 2024.

- **Hostility and lack of capacity within UU**: Derry's current university provider UU has traditionally promoted and developed its other three campuses – in Belfast, Coleraine and Jordanstown – at Magee's expense, earning the Derry college the unenviable tag of the 'fourth-priority campus of the North's second university'. By way of excuse, UU has traditionally blamed the 'MaSN cap', which restricts the maximum number of government-funded HE students in the North, while neatly ignoring the fact that it has continued to distribute those places it does have in its east-of-the-Bann campuses.

- **A recalcitrantly 'anti-Derry' civil service**: as recently as last year, a *Belfast Telegraph* Freedom of Information (FoI) request uncovered that in 2020 Department of Economy officials had drawn up an 'anti-Derry attack sheet' for unionist politicians opposed to university expansion in the North West. Sixty years ago, Department of Labour officials briefed Lockwood not to site the new university in Derry but instead bring it to Coleraine.

- **An opportunistic, Belfast-focussed political sector**: In February 2020 just one month after the two governments had sanctioned massive expansion at Magee, the minister signed off on a £126m bailout to complete UU's new Belfast campus and at the same meeting told the committee the Derry development would have to wait [as there was no money left].

A 2018 graphic from a Derry University Group submission to the Oireachtas, showing the annual income of third level colleges across the island. Magee's finances are controlled centrally by UU, giving the campus no independent income.

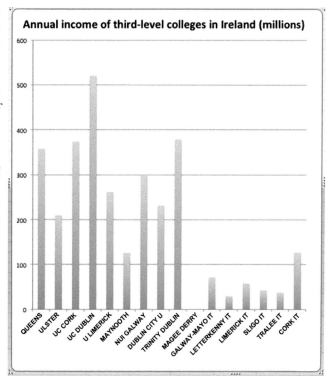

Annual income of third-level colleges in Ireland (millions)

- **Historical British inertia**: Westminster, the Northern Ireland Office and the Strategic Investment Board have traditionally adhered to unionist policies on NI. Plans to develop Belfast are readily funded and green-lit; Derry advancements are subject to delay and challenge.

- **Generational cynicism, distrust, pessimism and defeatism in the North West**

- **Compliant Belfast-controlled media**

- **Lack of political will and accountability.**

Capping all of this is the fact that there is no independent oversight for universities in the North – as there is in all the other jurisdictions in the islands. The HE sector here is effectively the Wild West. As such, the main HE providers, which are heavily dependent on government funding – have been largely permitted to do as they please, as long as they don't upset ministers or civil servants and continue to adhere to the Belfast-first policy. Move courses and departments out of Derry? No problem. Research conducted in 2015 showed that over the course of five years more than 110 courses at Magee, across a wide range of disciplines, had been shut down or transferred out of Derry. Psychology, sociology, history, languages, business courses all disappeared.

The defining insult was the decision to transfer Incore's undergraduate programme out of Magee in 2018 – so claiming for the capital a peace and reconciliation institute built almost exclusively on Derryman John Hume's legacy. It was the city's Elgin Marbles moment – Incore had been Magee's shining jewel, attracting guest lecturers such as Bill and Hillary Clinton, Romano Prodi and Kofi Annan. And its removal to Belfast, combined with a decision to remove the post of Provost from the Magee Campus, convinced more and more people who had been prepared to give UU a chance that an independent university in the North West was the only viable option.

EARLY CAMPAIGNING

John Hume's first foray into politics was in the early 1960s as chair of the cross-community University for Derry Committee. He, and the vast majority of people in the North West, unionist and nationalist alike, believed that the North's second university should and would be centred at the already-established Magee College in Derry.

Countless books, reports and research papers have been written about the iniquitous, sectarian decision to site the new university instead at Coleraine. *Derry: Countdown to Disaster* (Gill, 1986), by the former *Derry Journal* editor Frank Curran, is an authoritative insider's account.

Curran records that on New Year's Day 1963, the Derry Corporation published a manifesto in the *Derry Journal*, on how Magee should be developed, offering to subsidise the new institution out of council rates. He recounts how nationalist leaders saw the project as a real chance for 'rapprochement' with the Unionist state, which it believed, in the early stages at least, was backing the project.

The government appointed a committee – named after its chair Sir John Lockwood – to report on the university question. At that time, Stormont was pushing ahead with a new city in Craigavon, County Armagh, as part of its strategy to develop unionist strongholds in the East, while ignoring or deliberately under-resourcing nationalist-held regions in the West. And

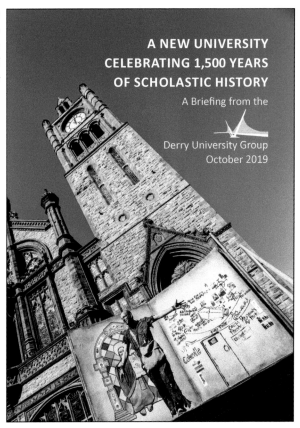

A brochure on the case for a new North West University presented by the DUG to representatives at Westminster in 2019.

A NEW UNIVERSITY CELEBRATING 1,500 YEARS OF SCHOLASTIC HISTORY

A Briefing from the

Derry University Group
October 2019

in keeping with that tradition, Derry's university campaign was secretly 'nobbled' by senior civil servants and senior unionists.

When Lockwood's recommendation, that the small unionist town of Coleraine was to be awarded the university, was duly announced there was uproar in Derry. In February 1965, more than 25000 people from the city took part in a massive 70-mile cavalcade from the North West to the steps of Stormont to protest the case. The Unionist parliament upheld Lockwood's decision, however, in what was widely regarded as one its most sectarian votes ever. Many observers, including John Hume, would later point to the university issue as the spark that lit the civil rights movement that would set the agenda in the North for the next three decades.

The Foyle MP and leading campaigner Eddie McAteer later told Frank Curran: 'I honestly thought that even Stormont would have to listen to the united voice of Derry; but not even I realised the depth the Stormont will to refuse justice to this city.'

When Curran's book, *Countdown to Disaster*, was launched in November 1986, he told Martin Cowley of the Irish Times: 'Eddie and John Hume both felt that the university was the point of no return. Eddie described it as "the point of despair". For Eddie it meant that all the parliamentary work of years had been useless. For Hume it meant that Stormont had to be challenged – possibly on the streets.'

CAMPAIGNING POST-GFA

Months after delivering the Good Friday Agreement in 1998, John Hume was again rebuffed and warned not to be a 'whinger' by the [then] University of Ulster when he demanded 10000 full-time students at Magee. It was becoming increasingly apparent that the post-Troubles 'peace dividend' was going to be a dividend for Belfast alone. The speed at which new developments such as the Titanic Quarter, the Gasworks, and the Waterfront were up-and-running stood in stark contrast to the situation in Derry, where the sites at Fort George and Ebrington have been left in abeyance for decades.

In the early 2000s, a new group of campaigners – including Pádraig Canavan, Philip O'Doherty, Garvan O'Doherty, Conal McFeely and Paul Gosling – formed the new University for Derry (U4D) group. They commissioned and launched a business case to develop Magee to almost 10000 students, and believed they had won the backing of both Stormont and UU. An apparent commitment was made in 2011, when a plan produced by the Stormont-constituted urban regeneration company, Ilex, to deliver 9400 students at Magee by 2020, was included as part of the NI Executive's Programme for Government.

To do this was going to require the University of Ulster transferring students from its other campuses to Derry. However, UU was already making plans to move its largest campus from Jordanstown into Belfast's Cathedral Quarter.

UU's former vice-chancellor Gerry McKenna predicted that this 'inordinately-expensive' plan was going to negatively impact Derry. Writing in *Fortnight Magazine* in 2010, he warned: "The recently-announced availability of the current Foyle and Londonderry College campus offers a tremendous opportunity for the University to complete its development

*University campaigners on the steps of Stormont in February 1965.
Included are the late Johnny and Ann McKane, whose son Damien is a prominent
campaigner today.*

*Sean Downey of FutureProof North West presenting a copy of the DUG's manifesto
to Paul McAuliffe at a special reception hosted by the Dublin Lord Mayor at the
Mansion House in November 2019.*

plan for the Magee campus. However, this will have to be achieved within a hugely-difficult financial environment and will require patience coupled with dedicated focus of purpose. It seems unlikely to be fulfilled if the University continues to pursue the inordinately-expensive, largely-unfunded, and academically-implausible, 'Jordanstown to Belfast' transfer plan. For some perplexing reason this particular 'elephant' remains stubbornly 'in the room'."

Professor McKenna would later go on to author the 2024 Royal Irish Academy report, recommending an independent North West University with Derry at its centre.

In 2013, as it became more and more apparent that the North West, and Magee, had again been misled (campus student numbers over the decade 2011 to 2020 would remain all but static), Conal McFeely set up the new Derry University Group (DUG) with Diane Greer and myself. Our initial objective was to fight for an independent university as a permanent legacy of Derry's successful City of Culture year, though, it rapidly became clear – particularly after Brexit – that a cross-border university model encompassing the entire city-region would be the most viable and robust option.

DUG researchers met with, and presented proposals to, British and Irish government representatives, and continuously lobbied locally and regionally. What was initially dismissed (by those who wished to silence Derry) as a fringe group quickly became an accredited, influential and effective lobby movement, involving hundreds of supporters and contributors from across the island and beyond. And the university issue slowly but surely returned to its rightful place at the top of the North West agenda. Info-billboards collated and designed by Kevin Hippsley of the DUG were displayed across the city – including the back of Free Derry Corner – and were featured widely in the media.

THE TIDE TURNS

Post-Brexit, the Irish government – and particularly the Foreign Affairs Minister Simon Coveney, who was a strong advocate for Derry – began taking more of a lead in the university issue. In 2018, the Oireachtas Joint Committee on the Implementation of the Good Friday Agreement sat at Ráth Mór in Creggan, and was receptive to a detailed briefing from the Derry University Group. The Taoiseach Leo Varadkar and his successor, and coalition partner, Micheal Martin subsequently both met university

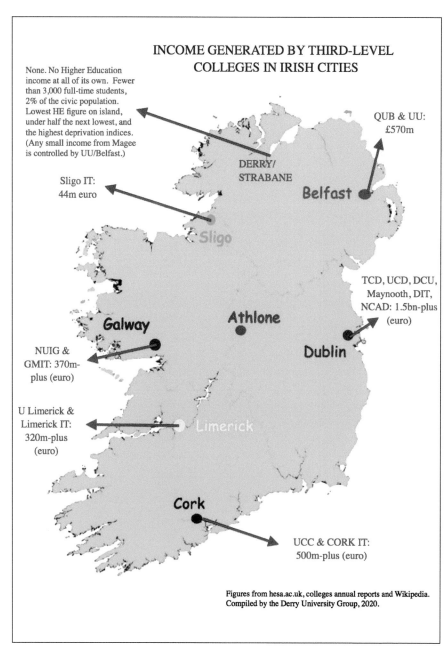

INCOME GENERATED BY THIRD-LEVEL COLLEGES IN IRISH CITIES

None. No Higher Education income at all of its own. Fewer than 3,000 full-time students, 2% of the civic population. Lowest HE figure on island, under half the next lowest, and the highest deprivation indices. (Any small income from Magee is controlled by UU/Belfast.)

DERRY/ STRABANE

QUB & UU: £570m

Sligo IT: 44m euro

Belfast

Sligo

TCD, UCD, DCU, Maynooth, DIT, NCAD: 1.5bn-plus (euro)

Athlone

Galway

Dublin

NUIG & GMIT: 370m-plus (euro)

U Limerick & Limerick IT: 320m-plus (euro)

Limerick

Cork

UCC & CORK IT: 500m-plus (euro)

Figures from hesa.ac.uk, colleges annual reports and Wikipedia. Compiled by the Derry University Group, 2020.

A DUG graphic from 2020.

campaigners at Ráth Mór. And Dublin's Lord Mayor Paul McAuliffe hosted a reception for Sean Downey's Derry expat group FutureProof North West and the DUG at the Mansion House in November 2019.

London was also taking notice. In June 2019, a visit to Derry and the North West was organised for senior MPs Mike Kane and Mike Amesbury, who both had connections with the city. And they were accompanied by Alison Stoecker from then Shadow Chancellor John McDonnell's office. During a packed schedule, the visitors met with the Derry University Group and learned about the issues surrounding the long-standing campaign for an independent university in the North West Region, led by the communities it would serve.

Labour MPs Mike Kane and Mike Amesbury, with special advisor Sarah Haughey, and Conal McFeely of the Derry University Group, during a visit to Derry and Donegal in 2019.

With the Stormont parliament in suspension, on returning to London the two MPs raised the university issue in the House of Commons, which led to a powerful intervention in the House of Lords, by Lord Andrew Adonis, calling for a new university to be established with its main campus in Derry.

In a speech in the upper chamber in January 2020, Adonis demanded that the British government draw up an action plan to develop a new university for Derry. He also castigated UU for its repeated failure to open the Derry Medical School promised in 2003 and described the (almost bankrupt) university's finances as 'shambolic'. Just days later, a new agreement was published by the British and Irish governments to reconstitute the suspended Stormont, a key component of which was the commitment to expand Magee to 10000 students by 2030.

Following the death of John Hume in August 2020, the Derry University Group called for the establishment of a cross-border university, centred in Derry, as a permanent legacy to the Nobel laureate – a call taken up and championed by senior Irish government TD Colm Burke. Subsequently,

The death of John Hume in 2020 sparked new calls
for a cross-border university in his memory.

Simon Harris, now Taoiseach, asked the Dublin Chamber of Commerce: "Why don't we have a cross-border university on the island of Ireland?... Education transcends borders."

The concept of a new cross-border institution – which would serve as a post-Brexit bridge between North and South – was beginning to gain currency. In 2021, the Royal Irish Academy (RIA) produced a series of reports on the future of Higher Education across the island in which it proposed the establishment of a cross-border university in the North West, from Sligo to Coleraine, with a Derry campus at its core. This was followed by a standalone Shared-Island funded report from the Academy in 2024, focusing on how a federal North West University could and would work.

Also in 2021, the DUG made submissions to the British government-led Levelling Up regeneration programme, and subsequently met with Department Permanent Secretary Sue Gray and the Northern Ireland Secretary of State Brandon Lewis. Later in 2021, Minister Lewis recommended improving the North West's university provision in a British government Command Paper.

He stated: "We are interested in the various possibilities for education to help reconciliation, through increasing integrated education, using technical and vocational education to improve educational outcomes for children across the community, and through improving Northern Ireland's university provision. An example of this might be a cross border university situated in the North West.

"This could symbolise the importance of North-South cooperation, representing an important step in achieving greater social cohesion and ensuring the North West receives the investment into social enterprises that it so richly deserves. Such an initiative could also help to address the longstanding issue of 'brain drain' in NI, add immediate value to NI's economy by providing more skilled jobs, and attract research funding and the promotion of businesses, helping to level up the least prosperous sub-region of NI."

The former Labour leader Jeremy Corbyn also supported the establishment of an independent university for the North West in January 2022, when he visited the city to mark the 50th anniversary of Bloody Sunday. The DUG had previously met, and received the backing of, his former Education spokesperson (now Labour Party Deputy Leader) Angela Rayner, at Westminster.

31. Of course, addressing the past and promoting reconciliation cannot be taken forward in isolation. Our proposals would take account of, and plug into, wider opportunities and initiatives that could help NI fulfil its potential as a safer, more tolerant, and more integrated society, aimed at helping future generations understand the past, each other, and their neighbours.

> **Case Study: the role of education in integrating and reconciling society**
>
> The slow process of reconciling and integrating a divided community is not achieved through one process or idea. It can only happen through gradual changes across all aspects of society. The education system, at all levels, plays a vital role in this. We are interested in the various possibilities for education to help reconciliation, through increasing integrated education, using technical and vocational education to improve educational outcomes for children across the community, and through improving Northern Ireland's university provision. An example of this might be a cross border university situated in the North West. This could symbolise the importance of North-South cooperation, representing an important step in achieving greater social cohesion, and ensuring the North West receives the investment into social enterprises that it so richly deserves. Such an initiative could also help to address the longstanding issue of 'brain drain' in NI, add immediate value to NI's economy by providing more skilled jobs, and attract research funding and the promotion of businesses, helping to level up the least prosperous sub region of NI.

In 2021, the Northern Ireland Secretary Brandon Lewis MP published a White Paper, including a recommendation that a cross-border university in Derry-Donegal could play a role in integrating and reconciling society here.

WHY A UNIVERSITY?

My late mother, Dr Áine Downey (d 2020), lectured at Magee from the 1960s to the 1990s – serving three different universities (Trinity, NUU and UU) from the same little office. Having campaigned for the new university in the 1960s with Hume and McAteer, she would later become the number one counsel to the Derry University Group. We hope very much that she would approve of this book.

Áine taught us the importance of a university – how it must become a leading and an integral part of society. It must foster new research, thinking and discussion, acting as the kernel for creativity, growth and improvement in all sectors from industry to social enterprise, and from education to health to government. It must become the heart and soul and voice – and economic driver – of its community.

This was something I witnessed in action as a student in Galway, and later in towns and cities across the island, when I served as Deputy President of the Union of Students in Ireland (USI) in the 1980s. The

University (College) of Galway would grow from 4,700 students in my time to more than 20000 today, with the city, its industry and regional economy, expanding alongside it. Limerick's National Institute of Higher Institute (NIHE) college would acquire full university status in 1989 and has quadrupled in size from 4000 to more than 17000 today. This is a pattern replicated not just along the Atlantic coast – which has also seen Cork, Tralee, Sligo, Mayo and Letterkenny develop apace – but right across the twenty-six counties, thanks to visionary strategy and investment from government and educationalists.

Derry has watched this growth and it has welcomed this growth. And importantly, Derry knows it is now time to deliver its own growth.

MEETING COMMUNITY NEED

Amie Gallagher, a community worker in Creggan and an active Derry University Group member – recently explained her rationale for supporting the campaign:

"As a mother and community worker it is disheartening to witness the lack of will to deliver appropriate university provision for the North West. Daily we see the effects of disadvantage and deprivation in our community. A university which has larger student numbers would attract investment and stimulate higher wage employment, benefitting everyone in our city.

"A new outward looking and progressive university, truly invested in this place and its people, could also seek to build on local assets, characteristics and unique experiences to create opportunities/courses, stimulate research/innovation and deliver solutions/spin-offs which address community need and are relevant to the North West, but attractive to students and businesses on a local and global basis.

"Many of the people we work with don't see third level education as a viable option for themselves or their children, primarily due to the financial burden. For those who can, they do so in the knowledge their young person is unlikely to return. For too long we have witnessed families export their children and futures and the damage this has done to family and community wellbeing, prosperity and cohesion over the generations.

"There are limited opportunities for the adults we support who return to education. To continue their education often means travelling to Belfast, often not possible due to childcare, work commitments, the cost of travel and lack of public transport infrastructure.

"I am a lone parent of a child with additional needs who would be unlikely to be able to live independently, especially away from home and their support network. They are academically able, but their future prospects are severely limited by the courses/places on offer at Magee.

"How do we explain to our young people that they are disadvantaged just because they are from Derry? They deserve to be able to reach their full potential and a have equitable choice in their education."

THE NEW RIA MODEL

Following the removal of the hard land border in Ireland in the mid-1990s, Britain's decision to leave the European Union in 2016 precipitated renewed debate on the continued viability of the political border here. Brexit opened opportunities for industries and businesses in the North, and saw a raft of new cross-border partnerships in health, education and, of course, commerce.

The massive historical affinity between Derry and Donegal – both of which suffered particular disadvantage and marginalisation – meant that, with the eradication of the physical trappings of Partition, the two counties began redeveloping closer and closer links.

In April 2022, in the run-up to the NI Assembly Elections, university campaigners unveiled billboards and a 'Wall of Protest' at various locations across the North West.

Professor Gerry McKenna of the Royal Irish Academy presents his report to the Derry University Group at Ráth Mór in June 2024.

The potential for solidifying a formal North West HE partnership was, as mentioned earlier, recognised by the Royal Irish Academy's Higher Education Futures Taskforce in 2021 as part of its series of discussion papers on developing tertiary institutions across the island. The Derry University Group made submissions to the research group and lobbied it. Scores of the island's top educationalists and administrators worked on the reports, including Professor Gerry McKenna and the Donegal academic Dr Eucharia Meehan, CEO of the Dublin Institute for Advanced Studies.

This was the first time that the viability of a cross-border university had been properly explored.

In 2022, the Dublin government's Shared Island fund then commissioned the RIA to produce a further report, specific to northwest Ireland, and the RIA partnered with the John & Pat Hume Foundation to carry out the research.

On April 30, 2024, the RIA published Finding Common Ground, Building Community, examining higher education policy and provision on both sides of the border in the North West. Of the two HE models considered for the region, the Academy favoured a new federal university over a HE cluster in the North West.

It stated: "The development of a federal cross-border tertiary education institution merits serious consideration. A federal cross-border tertiary education institution would be made up of existing constituent institutions but with an overall governance structure involving coordinated oversight of planning across the region, promoting collaboration and eliminating wasteful and unnecessary duplication. In such a scenario, each jurisdiction would continue to be responsible for the funding of its colleges and campuses."

The report described 'piecemeal' approaches to developing Derry and Donegal as 'wasteful and anachronistic', concluding: "The relative underinvestment in tertiary education in the greater North West has had major negative consequences for the development of the region. The rectification of this anomaly necessitates major joint affirmative actions by the Irish and UK governments and the Northern Ireland Executive. This should involve the development of a clear vision and programme to enable the region to fulfil its potential and find its niche within the economies of Northern Ireland and Ireland.

"...Ultimately, spatial planning of tertiary education and other development is a responsibility of governments. It is unrealistic and unfair to delegate such planning to tertiary institutions, which will, inevitably, have many competing pressures."

The Academy also called for independent scrutiny of the Northern Ireland university sector, the only HE sector on the islands without an oversight body.

The report stated: "It is difficult to envisage a HE oversight body supporting the current geographically skewed distribution of HE places or concluding that such concentration would be in the interests of economic and cultural development or social cohesion."

The Derry University Group holds that a new cross-border structure, dedicated to the development of the federal North West University, is the next necessary move for the governments. The RIA report is the most significant intervention in the NW university sector – and its economic sector – in a generation. If implemented, as it should be, alongside the Project Ireland 2040 Plan, the blueprint will transform both sides of the border in the North West.

The report must be the cornerstone of every economic discussion and development plan for the next decade. We commend Professor McKenna and the Academy for their vision and determination – and all those who have supported the 60-year campaign for a university for the North West.

This book will reference many of those who were prominent in the fight for what has been called the North's last remaining unresolved civil rights issue. Others, who helped keep the candle lit over the past 15 years – supporting, guiding and informing the campaign – and deserve particular thanks include: Jacqui Begley, Denis Bradley, Steve Bradley, Michael Canavan, Padraig Canavan, Tom Collins (*the Irish News*), Brónagh Crabtree, Brian Doherty, Michael Doherty, Gary Donnelly, Peter Doran, Emmet Doyle, Prof. John Doyle, Patrick Duffy, Mark J. Durkan, Mary Durkan, Colum Eastwood, Maurice Fitzpatrick, Amie Gallagher, Bert Gallagher, Paul Gallagher, Eamonn Gee, Philip Gilliland, Jane Grant, Shaun Harkin, Colin Harvey, The John & Pat Hume Foundation, Mo Hume, John Hume Jr, Anthony Hutton, Ursula Kelly, Barry James, Breandán Mac Suibhne, Joe Martin, Eamonn McCann, Pauline McClenaghan, Anne McCloskey, Paul McFadden, Damien McKane, Mary McKenna, Mitchel McLaughlin, Rosa McLaughlin, Sean McLaughlin, Úna McNally, Jackie McNamee, Denis Mullan, Mark Mullan, Garvan O'Doherty, Declan O'Kelly, Cónal Ó Míanáin, Ailbhe Ó Monacháin, Mark Patterson, Catherine Pollock, Thomas Pringle, Gerry Quinn, Julian Smith, Dr Bill Tormey, Trisha Ward, Terry Wright, and, of course, *the Derry News* and *the Derry Journal.*

We also remember the thousands who ran this campaign in the 1960s, right through some of this region's most challenging times. You continue to inspire as we carry out your mission, and we will not rest until your goals are achieved.

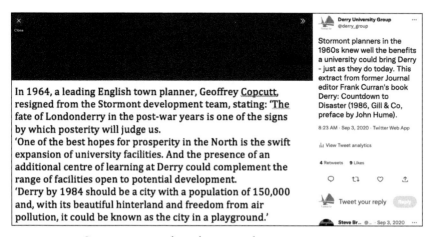

In 1964, a leading English town planner, Geoffrey Copcutt, resigned from the Stormont development team, stating: 'The fate of Londonderry in the post-war years is one of the signs by which posterity will judge us.

'One of the best hopes for prosperity in the North is the swift expansion of university facilities. And the presence of an additional centre of learning at Derry could complement the range of facilities open to potential development.

'Derry by 1984 should be a city with a population of 150,000 and, with its beautiful hinterland and freedom from air pollution, it could be known as the city in a playground.'

Derry University Group
@derry_group

Stormont planners in the 1960s knew well the benefits a university could bring Derry - just as they do today. This extract from former Journal editor Frank Curran's book Derry: Countdown to Disaster (1986, Gill & Co, preface by John Hume).

8:23 AM · Sep 3, 2020 · Twitter Web App

View Tweet analytics

4 Retweets   9 Likes

Tweet your reply

Steve Br... @... · Sep 3, 2020

Sixty years ago, independent town planners were warning Stormont about their discrimination against Derry.

PART I
Unlocking Derry's potential

By Garrett Hargan

As a proud Derry native I am all-too-familiar with the feelings of a disenfranchisement which have filtered through generations. The calculated and systematic disinvestment of Derry manifests in high unemployment rates and low wages.

That trend runs from before the 1960s – when people took to the streets in a collective demand for civil rights – to the present day. And discrimination against the second city, whether conscious, unconscious or both, has persisted post-Good Friday Agreement.

It begs the question, what has Stormont done for Derry? And, more specifically, what have nationalist and republican politicians done since taking their seats around the Executive table?

My generation has a lot to be thankful for.

My grandparents grew up in a city where they were marginalised because of their religion, whether that be the denial of equal voting rights or access to housing.

My parents grew up in a ghettoised city where freedom of movement was restricted during the Troubles. Killings were commonplace; explosions the norm. That type of society was abnormal and the scars run deep, physical, and in many cases mental.

Lives were needlessly lost. Trauma passed on. Yet peace offered a renewed sense of hope.

There can be no doubt the landscape of the city has improved. Today, the EU-funded Peace Bridge connects the traditionally-unionist Waterside to the predominantly nationalist Cityside.

Ebrington, a former British Army barracks handed back to the city, is now taking shape and could be a hive of activity in the not too distant future.

But, the biggest signifier that times have not *sufficiently* moved on is that the same debates the city was having about needing investment in the 1960s still persist to this day.

Integral to those debates, then and now, you have the Magee issue casting a shadow over the city. For decades it's been recognised as the key to unlocking the city's untapped potential.

John Hume led the university campaign in the 1960s. As chief organiser it was a hard lesson and political education when a decision was made to site a second university in Coleraine rather than Derry.

Hume would go on to be the key architect of the peace process. The peace he helped broker was to be the harbinger of opportunity and economic prosperity.

Why then has that not transpired for Derry? The east-west divide that was rigorously challenged in the 1960s is alive and kicking.

KEEPING UNIVERSITY REVENUE IN THE EAST

That point is underscored by the fact that, post-Good Friday Agreement, Belfast appears to have swallowed the peace dividend whole – no clearer than when it comes to higher education provision.

With the relocation of 15,000 students from Jordanstown to Belfast, the city secured 83% of NI's campus-based student population.

In turn, that allowed the North's capital to reap the benefits of close to one billion pounds worth of capital investment from universities and higher education institutions themselves from 2013-2023.

The east also dominates when it comes to inward investment, assisted by 70% of all Invest NI funding.

Critics will say, but that's because more people reside in the east. True, with one considerable qualification: that being that the state designed itself that way. Remember it was just 60 years ago that Craigavon was created as a city to bolster the east, while Derry's rail network was being closed down.

By retaining 83% of students in the capital, building the best infrastructure there, and telling investors Belfast is the only show in town, you are guaranteeing that more people relocate to the east for work.

The flip side of that is that by treating Derry like a small town and depriving it of a sizeable university, it ensures young Derry people will continue to move to Belfast for their studies, travel south to the Republic or take flight to Britain to enrol at universities there.

Around 70% of all young students from Derry study outside the council area. Research has shown that students often get a job close to where they've studied, so that means many never return to Derry. And, why would they, when opportunities are limited…?

Having that substantial higher education skills pipeline in Belfast makes it attractive for inward investment. Indeed, having a proportion of students which is in another realm compared to other capital cities across these islands (Ireland and GB) means it is the ONLY attractive option for potential investors.

POOR NORTH WEST INFRASTRUCTURE

All the while the second city is still waiting on the A5 Derry-Dublin road to be upgraded. The A6 Derry-Belfast is partially done but, without investment in other infrastructure in the North West, it simply serves as a faster route to transport young people out of Derry to Belfast for higher education and job opportunities.

Our railway service is minuscule: one single track to Belfast and its satellite towns. Coleraine has better services. And there are no connections to Letterkenny and into the west, nor between Derry and Strabane, and further south to Dublin.

Therefore, with the ill-favoured combination of poor infrastructural connections and substandard university provision, the second city is left floundering.

Cities of a similar size in the Republic of Ireland, such as Galway and Limerick, have 25,000 and 30,000 students respectively. This has helped shield their economies from any significant damage at times such as the Covid-19 pandemic.

One can only deduce that is because political decisions in the Republic have not been informed by a religious or sectarian bias, as still appears to be the case in Northern Ireland.

Even when money made its way to Derry, an independent review of Invest NI showed there was an over-reliance on 'client companies'.

That is the case in Derry where one large US company, Seagate, has absorbed around 30% of the city's total funding package from Invest NI over 20 years, a company which incidentally cut jobs in recent months.

Seagate is by all accounts a respected employer and one valued in the city. The point is, the Derry operation was set-up years prior to the Good Friday Agreement.

Derry, with a proper university should have attracted numerous large, well-paying companies by now. Furthermore, if it had university students the vast majority of local businesses would benefit from their custom.

The city's nightlife could be entirely transformed with 20,000 additional students living here. We could be a city that hosts several festivals a year which are every bit as successful as our world-renowned Halloween carnival.

THE GALWAY MODEL

It is to Stormont and, it has to be said, nationalism's shame, that the city which won civil rights for all in Northern Ireland has been, to a large extent, forgotten.

Galway City is the perfect place for Derry to model itself on. The cities are similar in size with around 85,000 residents in their settlement areas.

Derry must have the ambition to aim for a student population akin to Galway's. Setting a target of 10,000 with no timeline will not move us closer to that goal.

Put simply, the 10,000 target is out of date. There is no time to waste getting there, it has to be a short, sharp ascent.

While I appreciate 10,000 comes before 25,000, to constantly reference 10,000 makes those at Stormont think that is the end goal. Once achieved, they can revert to type and focus on Belfast.

Just because Stormont missed a target of delivering 9,400 students by 2020 does not mean Derry as a city should stand still and that target should remain in place as an upper limit. Belfast has sailed into the distance and the likes of Galway and Limerick will continue on their upward trajectory.

The university debate must be reframed and recalibrated. Belfast cannot have 83%, that needs to be rebalanced. Belfast can drive the east, Derry must be the captain of its own ship to drive the west forward.

At the current rate of growth it could be at least another 50 years before Derry reaches the 10,000 full-time students milestone.

While that may sound facetious, it is based on growth from 3,289 FT students in 2010/11 when Derry's One Plan regeneration project was announced to 4,681 in 2022/23 (if we are to accept UU's figures).

Let's look at Galway for inspiration, its Council hails the myriad benefits students have brought to the city:

"In a City where the current population is approximately 80,000 residents, students are a significant element of the local economy.

"The student and research community based in NUI, Galway deliver a significant cash injection into the local economy across a range of economic activity including rents, entertainment, food and beverage and so on, on a consistent basis every year.

"The knowledge economy centred around the University has acted as a stabiliser in the City's economy over the decades, often insulating local businesses from the worst of recessions that towns and cities elsewhere in Ireland have faced.

"It has also increased the attractiveness of the City as a local for Foreign Direct Investment and the output of quality graduates and R&D research facilities and relationships on campus have supported the development of a world recognised Medical Device Cluster in the City that now underscores employment of over 20,000 people.

"It has supported the rapid growth of Galway City in recent decades. The city's population has grown from 47,000 in 1986 to 86,000 recorded in the last census.

"There are intangible contributions from the University all across the City's society in terms of fostering the Gaeltacht status of the City, the Culture and environment."

There is absolutely no feasible reason that Derry could not replicate the success of Galway in the North.

We are a similarly compact city. We are a proud welcoming people, in an historic Walled City.

The difference is, Galway, with its student population has been given the tools and opportunity to carve out a place for itself as an attractive destination for business and tourism.

Let us ask ourselves why that hasn't been allowed to happen in Derry…

PART II
How it all began

The Stormont government knew that if a free vote were allowed in Stormont, the Lockwood Report would be cast aside. But the hidden forces of extreme Unionism were adamant that a prize like the university could not be permitted to go to Derry, where it might well create a radical and largely anti-Unionist atmosphere that would render the continuance of the gerrymander virtually impossible, and make unchallenged Unionist control of the North less certain. The government decreed that the party whip would be on all Unionist members. Not only that, but to underline the government stand, a vote of confidence in the government was allied to the motion asking for sanction of the Report. Unionist members were placed under severe pressure in the weeks leading up to debate days, 3 and 4 March 1965. O'Neill himself led the government speakers. He denied that there was discrimination against Derry. He rejected suggestions that the decision was politically inspired. No one in the government, he affirmed, had anything but respect for the qualities of the ancient, historic city. Labour's David Bleakley ___

An extract from Frank Curran's 'Derry: Countdown to Disaster',
explaining how the 'hidden forces of extreme unionism' stopped the
university coming to Derry in 1965.

To get a sense of perspective on the magnitude of the Magee scandal, it will help if we first take the reader back to its roots.

According to Tom Fraser's *History of Magee: Past and Present*: "The formal opening of Magee College took place on 10 October 1865 in a ceremony attended by the Moderator of the General Assembly of the Presbyterian Church, the largest Protestant denomination in the province of Ulster, and the Mayor of Londonderry, their presence acknowledging the College's theological origins and purpose and the sense of civic pride that had been instrumental in bringing it into being.

"...While the Church of Ireland could enjoy the facilities of Trinity College Dublin and from 1975 Catholics had their provision at Maynooth in County Kildare, training for the Presbyterian ministry could only be found after making the short sea crossing from Donaghadee to Portpatrick at one of the Scottish universities, with all the expense and inconvenience that this involved."

The College was intended to benefit not just the Presbyterian community, "but the material interests, as well as the social and intellectual advancement of Derry and the populous districts that surround it".

Seven professors were appointed (more than have been based at the college for the past decade) five of them clergymen. The college was the legacy of Mrs Martha Magee, the widow of a Presbyterian minister, whose sons had died. She left £20,000 – which she had inherited from her brothers – to endow the college, the location of which was approved by the Lord Chancellor of Ireland, in the face of a strong lobby from Belfast who wanted it there.

With the formation of the Royal University of Ireland, from 1881 Magee students were able to sit for a recognised university degree. Women students included the McKillop sisters, who founded what would later become the Londonderry High School for girls.

According to Fraser, "The Royal University had never really met Catholic aspirations and by 1906 its future increasingly came into question." The RUI split into two camps – Queen's Belfast and the new National University of Ireland (NUI), which would have colleges in Dublin, Cork and Galway. Magee refused to align with Belfast ("Belfast interests had never been sympathetic to Derry's aspirations") and instead linked up with Trinity College Dublin, which had opposed incorporation into the new NUI. Magee would thus remain an affiliated college of Trinity for the next sixty years.

During World War II, a massive underground bunker was developed at Magee for the Allied Command, which coordinated the Battle of the Atlantic from there.

Post-war the college thrived, and in 1960, Eddie McAteer – the Nationalist MP for Foyle in the Northern Ireland House of Commons raised the issue of siting a full university in Derry in a speech at Stormont. He was supported by the Derry Unionist MP Edward Jones – who would later be forced by his bosses to change his stance.

The university campaign proper got underway in 1962, and on New Year's Day 1963, the Derry Corporation published a manifesto of support in the *Derry Journal*.

In it they stated they would contribute to its running:

"The Council, as a tangible manifestation of its own convictions is prepared to sponsor a public foundation appeal and itself make an

annual contribution equivalent to the product of a threepence rate towards the finances of the university for a period of ten years from the date of its foundation."

Frank Curran, in his book Countdown to Disaster, noted: "The university issue created a city unity hitherto unknown… The campaign attracted many eager and able people from both traditions, in particular John Hume, a young school teacher at St Columb's College who was making his mark for his work in Credit Union activities and on social matters."

'AN ACT OF INTOLERABLE AUTOCRACY'

Derry genuinely believed that Belfast was finally going to do the right thing. Stormont appointed a committee to report on the university question, chaired by the English academic Sir John Lockwood. But by early 1965, the city had got wind that the Lockwood committee had been nobbled by Belfast unionist leaders and civil servants and that, whatever else happened, Derry was going to lose out. There was also, unbeknownst to the Derry lobby, a group of senior unionists from the city who were secretly working in collaboration with the Belfast establishment – the so-called 'faceless men'.

Hume was selected to lead the fight for Derry, alongside a cross-community committee which included Dr Desmond Sidebottom (Protestant), Brian Gallagher (Catholic), Michael Canavan (Catholic), solicitor Arthur Jack (Protestant) and Gerald Black (Protestant).

At a crammed public meeting in the Guildhall on February 8, 1965, convened by the unionist mayor Albert Anderson, Arthur Jack told the throng that if the university should be situated anywhere other than Derry, it would be because of "influence" and "not justice".

Three days later, John Hume met with Prime Minister O'Neill at Stormont. He later commented about that meeting: "We did not know of course that even as he listened to our appeal, the decision against Derry had already been taken."

A motorcade procession from Derry to Stormont on February 18, 1965 - effectively the first mass action of the civil rights movement – attracted 25000 people, but O'Neill would not bow.

The Lockwood committee was claiming that "the location of the university must be one in which development could proceed smoothly and successfully, unaffected by political considerations either at local or central government". Effectively, said Frank Curran, Derry and the west of the Bann were being punished further because of the corrupt unionist gerrymander.

Meanwhile, the unionist government at Stormont was under pressure from its own members – particularly from those in the North West – *not* to ratify the Lockwood report. So they enacted the party whip and called a vote of confidence in the government alongside the vote on the report.

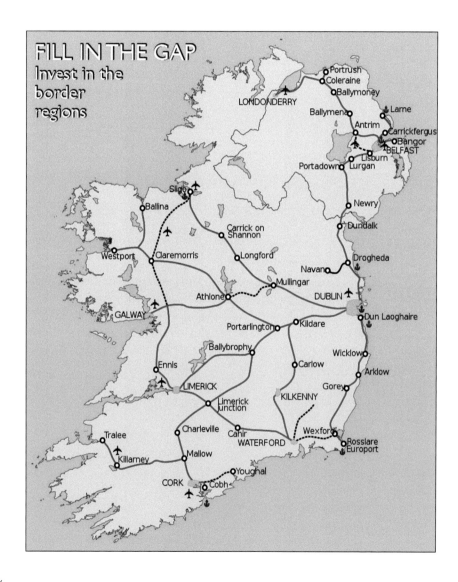

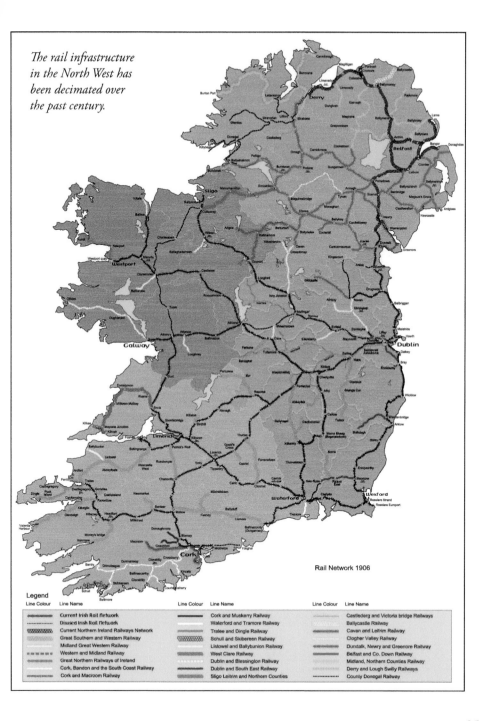

The rail infrastructure in the North West has been decimated over the past century.

Rail Network 1906

Legend

Line Colour	Line Name	Line Colour	Line Name	Line Colour	Line Name
	Current Irish Rail Network		Cork and Muskerry Railway		Castlederg and Victoria bridge Railways
	Disused Irish Rail Network		Waterford and Tramore Railway		Ballycastle Railway
	Current Northern Ireland Railways Network		Tralee and Dingle Railway		Cavan and Leitrim Railway
	Great Southern and Western Railway		Schull and Skibereen Railway		Clogher Valley Railway
	Midland Great Western Railway		Listowel and Ballybunion Railway		Dundalk, Newry and Greenore Railway
	Western and Midland Railway		West Clare Railway		Belfast and Co. Down Railway
	Great Northern Railways of Ireland		Dublin and Blessington Railway		Midland, Northern Counties Railway
	Cork, Bandon and the South Coast Railway		Dublin and South East Railway		Derry and Lough Swilly Railways
	Cork and Macroom Railway		Sligo Leitrim and Northern Counties		County Donegal Railway

O'Neill duly won his vote, but it was at a cost. His former attorney-general, Edmund Warnock, railed against what he called 'an act of intolerable autocracy…a shameful and shocking decision'.

Warnock commented: "It was political madness and the penalty will have to be paid by the people of Northern Ireland…Members are being forced to vote under duress and the decision of the House has no validity."

Hume said later that the denial of the university woke up the "political dormant" as to the nature of the Northern state. Speaking to Frank Curran, he commented: "The university decision electrified the people on the nationalist side, and I think [it] was really the spark that ignited the civil rights movement.

"When the university went to Coleraine, the chance of orderly change in Northern Ireland probably disappeared. It became clear to me certainly that the change could only be affected by positive political action."

In May 1965, Robert Nixon, the Unionist MP for North Down who voted against the Lockwood plans, said there were "nameless, faceless men" who had opposed building the university in their own city. Paddy Gormley, the Nationalist MP for Mid-Derry, then identified them as: former mayor Gerry Glover; Londonderry Sentinel editor Sydney Buchanan; retired Magee professor Rev RL Marshall, Magee lecturer Rev. John Brown; Dr W.R. Abernethy, Governor of the Apprentice Boys; local Unionist Association treasurer Robert Stewart, and Londonderry Unionist Association Secretary J.S. Bond. Nixon was expelled from the Unionist Party parliamentary group for his troubles.

It is impossible to quantify the enormity of the Lockwood decision on both Derry and Northern Irish history. Suffice it to say, it changed the entire history of the state – and is frequently cited as the single most specific sectarian act of a corrupted generation.

PART III
Post-Lockwood

As part of its recommendations that Coleraine would host the new university, Lockwood recommended the complete closure of Magee College. But the Derry campus would survive by the skin of its teeth, albeit in shadow form, as a small satellite campus of the New University of Ulster (NUU).

In 1972, as Coleraine struggled to attract viable numbers, undergraduate degrees were cut entirely from Magee – reducing it the status of "Institute of Continuing Education". The campus, run by a skeleton staff who were expected to give priority service to Coleraine [and later Jordanstown], remained innovative, however, and developed very successful professional courses, post-grad courses, community courses and programmes to get mature students back into education.

The merger of the NUU and the Ulster Polytechnic in the mid-1980s saw new physical development at Magee and the return of undergraduate provision, so by 1995 there was a combined total of 2500 full- and part-time students registered at the campus, its highest number ever.

That number started to drop again in the 1990s, however, after all capital development funding was re-routed to other campuses. And no less a personage than John Hume was warned to stop "whinging", when he again made the case anew for 10000 full-time students in Derry.

The then University of Ulster was keen to develop its Belfast footprint, and in 1993 it began planning a £70m campus in Springvale. The university would spend £10m before the futile project ultimately collapsed in 2002, sparking a full investigation by the NI Audit Office.

'TARGETED DELAY'
When the neglect of Magee is referenced, there is a need to distinguish between past and present. While the 1960s and 1970s saw direct and overt discrimination at play, the early 2000s saw 'targeted delay' used as the chosen weapon to stifle the campus.

Modern plans for expansion of Magee only started to come together again around 2008. That is due, in large part at least, to the dysfunctionality of Stormont.

Outsiders may think of the past twenty-five years of peace and assume the North had a functioning government throughout. Not so, it has been down for over a third of its existence.

One of those periods was between October 2002 and May 2007.

As the parliament reconvened, it seemed the foundations were being laid for Magee expansion again. And some people were high on the idea that, finally, Derry would be treated as the second city and an economic powerhouse for the north west region.

In 2009/10 Ulster University (UU) welcomed the official transfer of lands at Clooney to Foyle and Londonderry College saying it marked a "vital stage in its plans for major expansion" of the Magee campus.

Plans would include two new research institutes, rapid growth in student numbers and innovative new degree and study courses.

Magee's growth would also "significantly strengthen the campus's central role" in consolidating and developing Derry as a "knowledge city".

Professor Deirdre Heenan, then Dean of Academic Development at Magee, said the transfer of land would not only facilitate the creation of a "flagship education campus" but would also move development of Magee campus a step further to fruition.

"I am absolutely delighted, as acquisition of Foyle and Londonderry lands mean we will almost double our physical presence in the city and is a further reflection of our commitment to Magee campus," she said.

"Through this development, the University can realise its ambition to be a catalyst for economic, social and cultural regeneration in the North West. This is a fantastic day for everyone who has worked for an expansion of higher education in the city and region and an integral part in realising our ambitious plans for growth and expansion in the City.

"The College's migration to Clooney in the Waterside will free up 30 acres of much needed space for the growth of third level education in the city. When the College moves, the University intends to acquire vacated land at Northland Road and develop it as the centrepiece of Magee's expansion."

But a year later, in June 2011, the chair of Stormont's Employment and Learning committee warned that any expansion of third level education would be "unlikely" because of the deficit in the department's budget.

Basil McCrea's statement cast further uncertainty over the University of Ulster's plans to expand its Magee campus.

He said it was difficult to see how Magee could grow given the current financial climate.

"The higher education budget as it currently stands is going to be contracting rather than expanding," warned Mr McCrea. "The pressure will be on the University of Ulster to maintain its three university campuses, never mind expanding. So this is something that is going to be quite difficult in the medium term." (BBC NI report)

In September, the Minister of Employment and Learning Dr Stephen Farry scaled back expansion plans blaming "financial pressures". He added: "At this stage we're looking at a few hundred additional places."

'DERRY LET DOWN'

SDLP MLA Pat Ramsey who was on the Department of Employment and Learning committee said Derry had been let down: "I think it's shameful that we are at this stage. The applications to the Magee campus this year have been almost 5,000. The university could only take 1,000 people."

The supposed transfer of the lands at Foyle & Londonderry College on Northland Road to Magee, first mooted in 2003 and supposedly agreed in 2010, was only completed in 2019.

However, as of 2024, no development whatsoever towards the 'flagship education campus' referred to by Dr Heenan in 2010 has yet taken place, and the space remains a carpark.

Meanwhile the Magee Medical School, first promised by UU in 2003, was eventually opened in 2021 – after much resistance from Belfast. As of 2024, there is still no new dedicated building for the students who attend the school.

PART IV
The race to build Belfast

1963... Placard carrying students of Magee University College photographed with Mayor Gerald Glover before leaving for Stormont where they handed in a petition urging a university for Derry.

A Derry Journal clipping from 1963 showing the disparity in educational spending between Queen's and Magee. Sadly, the massive imbalance has changed very little.

In February 2012 news broke that the University of Ulster had bought up a large swathe of land in Belfast's north inner city to house a new '£250m' campus.

An Outline Business Case for the redevelopment of the University's Jordanstown Campus (approved in March 2010) had recommended relocating the majority of the activities and students from Jordanstown to a significantly expanded Belfast campus.

A similar £250m expansion plan for Magee had been proposed and considered at the same time but was shelved by UU. The university could not serve two cities.

Around 15,000 students were to be relocated from Jordanstown to the new Belfast campus. The building programme was hailed as the largest single investment in the university's history.

Yet over that period there appears to have been no great pressure exerted by the government or the civil service on Ulster University to move any students from the County Antrim campus to Derry. This was despite Magee's long-established need and the fact that Belfast already had a colossal percentage of the North's students. Significantly, there had been no call for, campaign for, or demand for a new Belfast campus, as there had been in Derry.

Back when the Lockwood Report was being drawn up, there was a recommendation that, to ensure regional balance, the second university should be sited at least 40 miles outside Belfast. There were, however, no such safeguards in place when UU decided, by itself, to move into the capital in the early 2000s. There does not appear to have been external scrutiny of the plan by any independent HE oversight commission.

Detailed plans for the development were submitted to the Department of the Environment, and the Education and Learning Scrutiny Committee at Stormont was briefed on the plan.

Committee chair Basil McCrea, who previously couldn't envisage any expansion at Magee, now seemed to have resolved his concerns about the shortfalls in the HE budget, describing the plans as "astonishing".

He enthused: "It's fantastic, it's great. Breathtaking is what you'll see when you see the plans unveiled. It's a really good thing for north Belfast and the whole city." (BBC NI report)

He said, in theory, the plans could be approved in six months, with work beginning by the end of the year.

If only the same urgency had been applied to investment at Magee.

And like that, the ball was rolling to inject life into what has become a neglected part of Belfast City Centre.

BOOMTOWN

In April 2014 a private developer submitted an application to build a nine-storey, 200-bedroom student accommodation block next to the University of Ulster's proposed new Belfast campus.

Numerous student accommodation blocks followed – 5,000 student units have been built in Belfast since 2016 with another 3,773 in planning.

A multi-million pound investment was announced to improve the area from Castle Place to the new Ulster University campus on York Street, as part of wider plans to rejuvenate the entire city centre.

This is just a snapshot of the investment that was pumped into Belfast due to UU's decision to move all 15,000 students a few miles.

Since then U.S. President Joe Biden has spoken at the campus (April 2023). One principle applies for Belfast and an entirely different one for Derry.

'NO REGRETS'

Ulster University still stands over the decision to move all Jordanstown students into Belfast, as do our Ministers.

Speaking in Derry in 2024, Economy Minister Conor Murphy said that investment had been "transformational" for Belfast. No mention was made that almost £1 billion had been given to Belfast for Higher Education capital building from 2013 to 2023 while just £25m was given to Derry over the same period.

Neither UU nor our Ministers seem to have considered that, if 5,000 of those students had been relocated to Derry, it would have taken student numbers here up to close to 10,000. They certainly did not give voice to any concerns.

If that had been done, Belfast could still have 40,000 campus-based students as well, about 75% of NI's student population. That 75% would still have been far and above what any other capital has on these islands, with Dublin having around 40%, London 23%, Edinburgh 27% and Cardiff 37%.

With 10,000 students Derry would have a fairer share of the North's total, with approximately 19%.

The North is a small place, therefore Derry should be the economic driver in the west, just as Belfast is in the east. To do that, Derry needs a higher percentage of students.

UU BELFAST OVERSPEND

The UU Belfast campus was initially expected to cost £254m and was to open to students in September 2018.

By 2022, that figure had risen to £364m, according to an audit office report – with the final number expected to be even closer to £400m. That is well over £100m over budget.

The Department for the Economy has contributed £41m of capital grants to the project and the Strategic Investment Board (SIB) facilitated the provision of Financial Transactions Capital (FTC) loan funding for the project totalling £174.325million, on behalf of the Department.

No such loan has been given to any other campus.

SIB is an non-departmental public body (NDPB) of The Executive Office (TEO), which, whilst not providing funding to UU, provided Grant in Aid to SIB to enable them to provide the FTC loan funding to UU.

Therefore, the office of the First and deputy First Minister had a significant hand in funding the Belfast campus.

No such special dispensations were made for Magee.

Belfast Telegraph @ @BelTel · Aug 21
Belfast's water and sewage system cannot cope with plans for massive student accommodation block

belfasttelegraph.co.uk
Belfast's water and sewage system cannot cope with plans for massiv...
Major problems with Belfast's water system have resurfaced, after plans were submitted for what would be the largest student ...

No new course places without living spaces

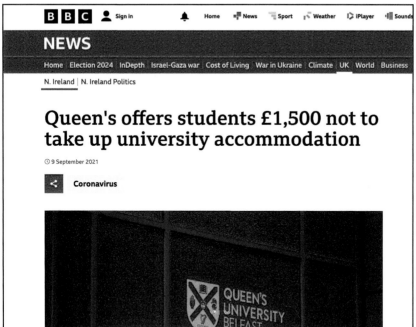

NEWS

Home | Election 2024 | InDepth | Israel-Gaza war | Cost of Living | War in Ukraine | Climate | UK | World | Business

N. Ireland | N. Ireland Politics

Queen's offers students £1,500 not to take up university accommodation

9 September 2021

Coronavirus

There are increasing signs that Belfast – now home to more than 80 percent of all NI university students – has become unmanageably overheated.

PART V
The long, slow death of the 'One Plan'

After the building moratorium of the 1990s and early 2000s, which followed the brief hope of the UU merger years, modern expansion proposals for Magee were once again mooted in 2008. These culminated in the One Plan, which would be published by the Derry Urban Regeneration Company Ilex in 2011.

The supposedly-transformational One Plan was centred on the premise that the government would deliver 9,400 full-time students at Magee by 2020. Initially, the plan – which included proposals to regenerate vacated British army sites at Fort George and Ebrington – had massive buy-in from the North West community. Indeed, it would become the linchpin of all local (and national) government economic and development strategy in the North West for the best part of a decade.

But the ink wasn't dry on the paper before ministers and civil servants in Belfast began working to undermine its contents.

The One Plan was included in Stormont's 2011 Programme for Government (PfG). However, the Department of Employment and Learning (DEL) Minister Stephen Farry, who had responsibility for higher education, would later that insist that only the regeneration of Fort George and Ebrington were specifically mentioned in the PfG – i.e. Magee expansion had dropped off the table.

Foyle MLAs duly continued to argue the case for Magee expansion at Stormont well into the late teens, however, implying that they were either being misled or strung along.

Incidentally, after being handed back to the city in the early 2000s, the Ebrington site is only now beginning to achieve some degree of potential, while Fort George is essentially wasteland except for one innovation building.

PART-TIME, FULL-TIME AND GHOST STUDENTS

The Magee campus – according to UU's figures – has a combined total of approximately 5,000 full and part time students, with the 10,000 target as far away as it was in 2014.

However, that figure of 5000 is strongly disputed by the Derry University Group, who believe the real number to be considerably lower and are demanding that UU publishes specific course breakdown figures. The campaigners claim many students are nominally registered at Magee and then required to study at one of the bigger campuses. On one occasion, UU actually published figures suggesting that more than 9000 students were registered at Magee, before being forced to explain that they had mistakenly included thousands of students who had merely been sitting entrance exams at the campus.

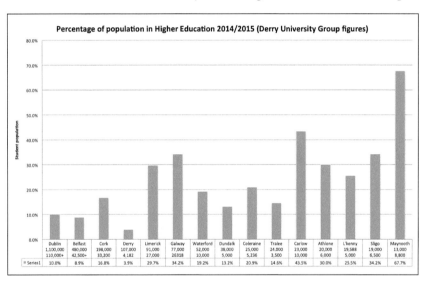

Each full-time student is estimated to contribute £20,000 per annum to their host regional economy.

A big issue here is that scrutiny of the HE sector in Northern Ireland is much more ineffective than elsewhere on the islands – a factor emphasised by the Royal Irish Academy in two different reports – 2021 and 2023.

From 2008/09 there was, seemingly, a mini jump in combined part-time and full-time numbers at Magee from 3,568 to 4,032 in 2009/10. That rise of 464 students was split pretty evenly between full-time and part-time students.

It is important to note that at that stage a third of all students studying at Magee were part-time.

A Freedom of Information response showed that, again according to UU, that combined figure rose to a high of 5,098 students in 2014/15.

The problem is at least 25% of those students were registered as part-time, that is not a split any university wants when it comes to students and explains why the Magee campus never felt busy even at that peak.

Furthermore, part-time students who do not relocate for their studies and are rarely on campus do not benefit the city much in an economic sense.

For instance, if we look at Queen's University Belfast in that very same year, it had 20,151 students and only 2,719 (13%) were part-time.

MISDIRECTION?

Prior to ruling out the One Plan strategy for Magee expansion, ministers again resorted to what appear to have been delaying tactics – the old familiar 'you need a business case' ploy.

In September 2014, Sinn Féin MLA Maeve McLaughlin was pressing the DEL Minister about a business case for Magee expansion. She said: "The Minister for Employment and Learning gave clarity on the need for a business case, which was causing some confusion in the city and beyond."

At that stage, Minister Farry stated: "If a proposal were to be taken forward to expand the Magee campus in line with the vision set out in the One Plan, then a full economic appraisal would be required."

Ms McLaughlin made clear Magee expansion was a critical catalyst project in the One Plan and stated that it included [the addition of] 6,000 full-time undergraduate students over the ten-year period to 2020. Others in Derry, not surprisingly, were of the firm opinion that the One Plan had been a business case in itself.

She added: "They are also about securing a 1,000 increase in the maximum student number (MaSN) by 2015, doubling the MaSN by 750 full-time undergraduate students to 1,500 over the 10-year period to 2020 and, equally, accelerating the development of the C-TRIC facility."

At that time, figures showed Derry had the lowest level of higher education (HE) provision of any major city on the island of Ireland.

Derry's students represented 2·9% of the resident population, while those in Belfast, Cork, Limerick, Dundee or Lincoln made up 9·6%, 15·8%, 20·6%, 14·1% and 13·6%. [See graph]

SDLP MLA Pat Ramsey said: "The One Plan encompassed, consulted and surveyed every household in the city. As a result, the key economic driver for the importance of Derry and its regeneration — culturally, socially and every other way — was the Magee campus. It was adopted with great aplomb by the First Minister and the deputy First Minister coming to the city and welcoming it.

"It was in the Programme for Government, but I am sure that the Minister will tell us that Magee was not specifically identified in that document.

"...In the Programme for Government, and given that the One Plan was key, certainly for representatives of the North West, how many times did the Office of the First Minister and deputy First Minister seek an update on the progression, development or out-workings of the One Plan, as it was identified to Maeve or myself? I would be keen to hear that from the Minister."

'NO BUSINESS CASE REQUIRED'

Ulster Unionist Derek Hussey also spoke in favour of Magee expansion.

He said Mr Farry was "effectively saying that the proposed expansion of the University of Ulster's Magee campus was off the table due to the Northern Ireland Executive Budget cuts."

Mr Hussey pointed out that in a similar Adjournment debate in September 2013, his colleague Sandra Overend asked a very salient question that cut to the heart of the question:

"...the Minister has said that no business case is needed, and the Magee provost, Dr Heenan, also said that detailed costings are not being sought. So, we need to have clarity on the expansion. We in the House are all aware that budgets are stretched throughout all Departments, and the higher education budget, I am sure, is no different." [Official Report, Vol 87, No 6, p63, col 2].

But in 2014, just one year on, the Minister said a business case would be necessary for Magee expansion.

"I want to address the specific issue of whether a business case is, indeed, required. In the context of a specific proposal on a stand-alone basis to expand Magee, we would need a business case for that purpose.

"For what we have adopted to date, which has been a policy of incremental growth of university places that adopts a pan-Northern Ireland approach, albeit, I have to confess, with a certain skewing towards the University of Ulster and Magee, we do not need a business case to proceed."

He concluded: "I stress that, without a business case, incremental growth can still continue." — [Official Report, Vol 87, No 6, p66, col 1].

In other words – you won't get anything at all if you rock the boat.

'9,400 A STARTING POINT'

Colum Eastwood, then an MLA, said 9,400 full-time students was "a compromise, a starting point – Unless we get at least to that point, we have no chance of redressing some of the difficulties that we face."

Yet ten years later the target has not changed.

Speaking then, Eastwood added: "Census figures relating to employment were revealed in July and were revised this month. They showed that there are 15,000 more jobs in the four Belfast constituencies than there were in 2009 just after the financial crash.

"However, the picture in Derry is very different: in the same period, we lost nearly 2,000 jobs. Derry is supposed to be alongside Belfast and, as part of the economic strategy, one of the major places that we look at for economic expansion.

"Derry's employment figures are contracting, so, for us, the issue around Magee is not just, as Pat Ramsey said, that we want more Derry people to go to university. It is a fundamental economic issue that needs to be resolved, but it just never has been resolved. We need the proper number of students doing the proper kind of high-tech courses."

The Derry University Group would subsequently publish research – and billboards – based on the disparity in growth between Derry and Belfast after the Good Friday Agreement.

Researcher Cormac Duffy's key findings – drawn from NI government statistics accrued in 2015 – showed:

- The Belfast economy had grown by 14% in real terms since the Good Friday Agreement (GFA)

- The Derry economy had contracted by 7% in real terms since the GFA

- Belfast income per capita had grown by 14% in real terms since the GFA

- Derry income per capita had fallen by 12% in real terms since the GFA

- Belfast was among the top 20% of UK government districts for economic performance since 1997

- Derry was among the bottom 5% of UK government districts for economic performance since 1997

- Per capita income in Belfast was over £31000 in 2015

- Per capita income in Derry was £15000 in 2015 – less than half of that of Belfast.

'GENERAL COMMITMENT'

In 2014, DEL Minister Stephen Farry said there was a "general commitment" to the One Plan in a Programme for Government.

However, he continued: "Only the regeneration of Fort George and Ebrington are specifically mentioned. Importantly, my Department is not measured or scrutinised in relation to the expansion of Magee in any respect.

"When I assumed office in May 2011, there was no Executive budgetary commitment or resources within my departmental budget to facilitate the expansion of Magee. However, through two bids to the Executive — the first arising out of the tuition fee settlement and the second relating to the jobs and economy initiative — and from redirecting resources in my pre-existing budget, I have been able to expand higher education by around 1,600 places across Northern Ireland, with 1,200 being directed to our universities.

"The University of Ulster has received more than its proportionate share of those places, receiving 652. In line with its stated commitment, the university has allocated those places to the Magee campus. So I do believe that solid and steady progress was being made towards the interim target of 1,000 additional places by 2015 as set out in the One Plan, before budgetary uncertainty and now cuts have forced a pause in our expansion plans."

"I appreciate that the Derry/Londonderry strategy board is developing a business case in relation to the much greater proposed expansion of the Magee campus in line with the One Plan target through to 2020. The business case is required, given the location-specific nature of the proposal. We have received the needs-analysis aspect of the business case, with the remainder expected to arrive during the autumn.

"However, we are receiving this business case at a time when the Executive is facing an unprecedented budgetary crisis. My departmental budget has already been cut in-year by 4·5%. The previously indicated level of cuts to be formally ratified in the October monitoring round may well be exceeded. Furthermore, we are staring into the abyss, with even greater levels of cuts facing us in future years unless there is a major reassessment of the approach being adopted on some critical financial and policy matters in the Executive.

"I have had no alternative but to pass on 4% cuts in-year to our universities, with further uncertainty over forthcoming budgetary periods. My first responsibility is to work with the universities to manage the pressures as strategically as possible, with a particular focus on the direct needs of the local economy and the steps necessary to maintain international standards.

"I am sympathetic to the potential further expansion of the Magee campus of the University of Ulster, but I cannot be expected to both cut public spending and increase it at the same time within the context of higher education; it simply does not add up. Indeed, it is worth stressing that the resourcing of the One Plan's student numbers would represent a significant challenge in terms of funding and would require an investment of over £30 million on a recurrent annual basis."

Effectively, the minister was giving with one hand and imposing cuts with the other, all the while ruling out the chance of full expansion as per the One Plan.

So to recap, in Stormont in 2015, Sinn Féin MLA Maeve McLaughlin asked about a timeline for the One Plan. Ten years ago Foyle representatives were fighting the corner on this issue. Indeed, the SDLP's Pat Ramsey said it should have come before the Executive. So, why didn't it?

At Magee on 22 March 2024 to announce the taskforce for Magee. Minister Murphy announced with pride steps taken by the Executive to provide £150m in capital funding for the Strule campus in Omagh.

Again, why was no such intervention forthcoming for Magee after the One Plan was announced?

SHIFTING GOALPOSTS

In January 2016, UU and Derry City & Strabane District Council announced a new partnership drive to develop Magee – this time by 2025. The can was being kicked down the road. Where Maeve McLauglin and Pat

Ramsey were talking about 9,400 students by 2020, the deadline was now being changed to 2025.

This new proposal included increasing full-time undergraduate places by 2,636 bringing the total to 6000 by 2024. A partnership with the North West Regional College would achieve an additional 750 full time undergraduate places by 2024.

Council, in partnership with Ulster University, submitted its revised outline business plan for the expansion of Ulster University's Magee campus, with the primary objective of reinforcing and growing Derry's reputation as a "vibrant" University city.

Mayor of Derry City and Strabane District Council and Chairperson of the Strategy Board, Councillor Elisha McCallion, said: "We have a truly world-class, internationally focused institution at the heart of our city. It is our collective responsibility to ensure that it flourishes and is accessible.

"This is an opportunity to build upon the transformational journey that the city and district has been on over the last number of years."

'WE HAVE TO BE REALISTIC'

By November 2016, the new Stormont Executive was already issuing a shortfall warning.

Former Minister Farry stated: "We [also] have to appreciate that the expansion of Magee was not a formal commitment in the previous Programme for Government. People think it was: it was not. During the last mandate, we managed to expand Magee by several hundred places — about 650, to be accurate — and we have commenced the construction of the new £10 million teaching block, but this remains a long way short of the 10,000 additional places that people are looking for in the One Plan and, more recently, the strategy group under the city council in partnership with the university.

"We…have to recognise that we currently have a £55 million deficit in higher education. Before we can talk about expansion, we need to fix the hole first and make sure that the foundations are solid. When we published the Big Conversation paper in March this year, we talked about not just addressing the funding shortfall but looking to expand the number of places available in Northern Ireland in line with the needs identified in the skills barometer. Obviously, Magee can capture some of that, but more and more capital investment will be required to make this a reality."

University campaigner Terry Wright with Catherine Pollock and Garbhán Downey at the June 2024 RIA presentation at Ráth Mór.

Many of the Stormont parties found it wasn't always possible to keep a three-line whip on Magee expansion – even those which were openly supporting it.

Assembly minutes show that on 9 November 2015 Sinn Féin MLA Pat Sheehan objected to Irish Language being moved to Derry out of Belfast.

Minister Farry stated: "As a result of the budget cuts to my Department, Ulster University has sought to rationalise its course offerings across campuses, which has resulted in the decision to close some courses and to consolidate others. This includes the consolidation of Irish courses at the Magee campus. A bachelor's degree in Irish language and literature will continue to be offered at the Belfast campus as a part-time study option. The university has advised that, in making these decisions, a number of factors have been taken into consideration, including student demand, attrition rates, student satisfaction, employment statistics and research performance. Consolidation of teaching provision across all campuses will facilitate budgetary savings without impacting on the quality of teaching, which remains paramount."

Mr Sheehan: "Go raibh maith agat, a Cheann Comhairle. Gabhaim buíochas leis an Aire as an fhreagra sin. I thank the Minister for his answer. Does he agree that Belfast's reputation as the Irish language capital of Ireland has been built on the phenomenal foundation of Ulster University in York Street? Does he accept that it is a blow to the city and its reputation for this course to have been ended?"

Dr Farry: "It is important to clarify that the course has not been ended: the university has sought to consolidate its full-time provision in the Irish language at the Magee campus in Derry. Without wishing to intrude on internal Sinn Féin politics, I was under the impression that people were keen to see the expansion of the university at Magee and certainly to build up Magee's impact in taking forward a number of courses. Obviously, Magee is not that far from Belfast, and, as we expect students to travel to Magee for a range of other courses, particularly as courses are consolidated, the provision for Irish language should not be any different. It would be nice, of course, to have a situation in which the full-time provision was available in Belfast and Derry, and the Member will be fully aware of the context in which the decisions have been taken: cuts to the higher education budget. In the context of an improved situation, I hope that the university's approach could be reconsidered, and we could see the restoration of some full-time provision in Irish language in Belfast. As we look to the development of a Gaeltacht quarter in Belfast, for example, a certain logic and synergy could be developed. I certainly would not be disparaging about the fact that course provision is going to Derry, and I encourage the Member to recognise the difficult decisions that the university has been taking and the fact that it has, in the main, preserved Irish language provision overall."

In early 2017, Sinn Féin pulled out of the Executive citing DUP corruption, forcing the collapse of the institutions.

Ulster University: Total Student Population History by Campus 2009/10 - 2018/19										
	2018/19	2017/18	2016/17	2015/16	2014/15	2013/14	2012/13	2011/12	2010/11	2009/10
MAGEE										
Full-time	3,429	3,428	3,555	3,387	3,833	3,570	3,473	3,389	3,289	3,009
Part-time	884	790	783	1,004	1,265	1,149	993	793	859	1,023
Campus total	4,313	4,218	4,338	4,391	5,098	4,719	4,466	4,182	4,148	4,032
UNIVERSITY TOTAL	24,025	23,986	24,258	25,059	26,969	26,745	26,642	25,460	25,339	25,428

Source: Internal University Statistics

Derry was promised an extra 6,400 full-time students over the decade 2010-2020. It got 400. Belfast, already overheated, was promised none but would wind up with 15,000 more.

PART VI
'Anti-Derry attack sheet'

Despite countless promises, plans and strategies, the decade 2010 to 2019 ended with an increase of fewer than 300 full-time students at Magee.

However, in January 2020, Derry university campaigners scored a significant victory when the British and Irish governments guaranteed major Magee expansion as part of a new agreement to get the institutions up and running again.

Ulster University gets £126m bailout loan approved for campus

By Fiona McIntyre

Share

Just a month after Derry university expansion to 10000 students had been signed off in New Decade New Approach, the Department of Economy refused to hear a case for Magee and chose instead to spend £126m bailing out the near-bankrupt new UU Belfast campus.

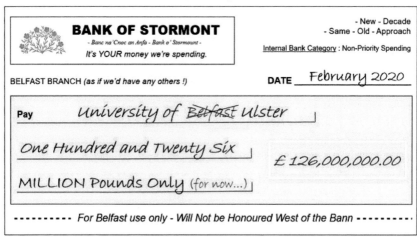

- New - Decade
- Same - Old - Approach

BANK OF STORMONT
- *Banc na'Cnoc an Anfa - Bank o' Stormount -*
It's YOUR money we're spending.

Internal Bank Category : Non-Priority Spending

BELFAST BRANCH *(as if we'd have any others !)*   DATE ___February 2020___

Pay   *University of ~~Belfast~~ Ulster*

One Hundred and Twenty Six   *£ 126,000,000.00*

MILLION Pounds Only (for now...)

‑ ‑ ‑ ‑ ‑ ‑ ‑ ‑ ‑ For Belfast use only - Will Not be Honoured West of the Bann ‑ ‑ ‑ ‑ ‑ ‑ ‑ ‑ ‑

As part of the New Decade, New Approach deal, Dublin and London confirmed that Magee would have 10000 full-time students by 2030 and that the medical school first promised in 2003 would open at last.

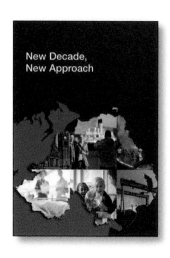

It stated, inter alia: "The Executive will expand university provision at Magee in line with commitments made by the previous Executive, including through the establishment of a Graduate Entry Medical School…

"The Executive will bring forward proposals for the development and expansion of the UU campus at Magee College, including the necessary increase in maximum student numbers to realise the 10,000 student campus target and a Graduate Entry Medical School."

Within a month, however, the DUP-led Department of Economy – which now held responsibility for higher education – finessed the North West again. At the first meeting of the committee post-suspension, a proposal to give a bailout loan of £126m to UU for its massively-over-budget new Belfast campus was approved.

At the very same meeting, a proposal to expand Magee in line with the New Decade New Approach principles was refused – on the grounds that there was no business case.

North West campaigners were furious. Effectively, the entire HE capital budget for the next Stormont parliament had all but disappeared in one dirty stroke.

It is incredulous that a power-sharing government with republicans and nationalists around the table could allow this to happen.

The DUP – which held the Economy Department from 2007 to 2022 – was widely blamed. Successive Economy ministers and civil servants have indeed opposed expansion, and the documents exist to prove it.

When the Department for the Economy (DfE) was challenged while under the ministerial control of the DUP, it is noteworthy that it had no plan to expand Magee, despite there being an intergovernmental, all-party agreement to do so in New Decade, New Approach.

The same tired lines were trotted out on countless occasions: "While specific priorities for higher education during the new mandate have yet to be decided, the Department, in partnership with others, is committed to further investment at all of the higher education institutions' Londonderry, Coleraine and Belfast campuses."

The DfE said resource distribution was entirely up to UU: "Northern Ireland's universities are responsible for their own course provision, including decisions regarding the distribution of allocated student numbers, and the campuses at which courses are based."

It was the perfect arrangement – UU was allowed to call the shots, while its friends in the Department and on the executive made sure Belfast developments would always get funding first.

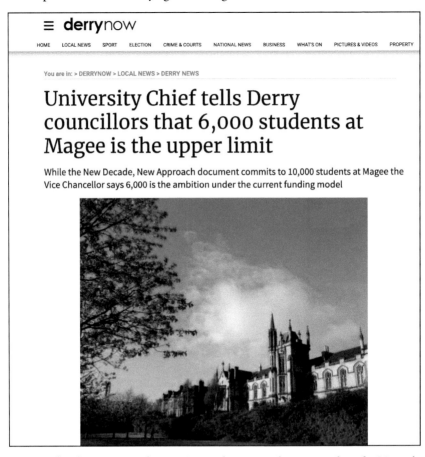

Just months after New Decade New Approach sanctioned 10000 students for Magee by 2030, UU bosses were saying they couldn't deliver it.

The Department insisted: "Students are the decision makers as to where they wish to undertake their studies be it at Belfast, Londonderry, Coleraine, Great Britain, the Republic of Ireland or other international destinations."

It was the perfect smartass answer. Course provision and infrastructure were nothing to do with the Department. But no-one ever thought to point out that students can't go where there are no buildings and courses.

When asked whether the lifting of the Maximum Student Numbers (MaSN) cap would have to be done to favour Derry, in another condescending response the Department said: "The dynamics of expansion and distribution of student numbers by universities is much more complex than simply increasing the cap on student numbers and course distribution. Students have a choice in where they wish to study."

Interestingly, that language would change when a nationalist (Sinn Féin) minister took up office in 2024. Conor Murphy said: "The expansion of Ulster University's campus in Derry is key to promoting regional balance, in line with my economic vision. Increasing the city's student population will be a catalyst for economic development in the North West region."

We wait in hope.

Investment

xii. The Executive will bring forward proposals for the development and expansion of the UU campus at Magee College, including the necessary increase in maximum student numbers to realise the 10,000 student campus target and a Graduate Entry Medical School.

xiii. Support for City Deal packages for Derry & Strabane and Belfast and the bid being developed by Mid-Ulster; Armagh City; Banbridge and Craigavon; and, Fermanagh and Omagh Councils.

xiv. Plan to complete both the Regional and Sub Regional Sports Stadia Programmes.

An extract from New Decade New Approach, published January 2020.

OPEN OPPOSITION TO DERRY EXPANSION

Opposition to expansion from within the Department and from the DUP was open and unrestrained, even after New Decade, New Approach was signed.

When a decision was made to move Allied Health undergraduate courses to Derry instead of Coleraine, the former Economy Minister publicly reprimanded the Ulster University Vice Chancellor. In March 2021, Diane Dodds said: "I met with the Vice-Chancellor of Ulster University on 3rd February, following his announcement on the future relocation of undergraduate health science courses to the University's Magee campus.

"I made it very clear to him that as a multi-campus university, dependent on funding from my Department, that I expect the Ulster University to be transparent and equitable in its distribution of teaching provision across all of its campuses.

"I have requested sight of the University's strategic plans to consider its proposals for future growth at its Coleraine campus."

Significantly, there was no such demand for equitable distribution when 15,000 students were being moved from Jordanstown into Belfast.

Prior to becoming Economy Minister himself, DUP MLA for East Antrim Gordon Lyons wrote to the department in March 2020, without a hint of irony, sharing the 'concern' of a single constituent that Allied Health courses would be moved to Magee instead of Coleraine.

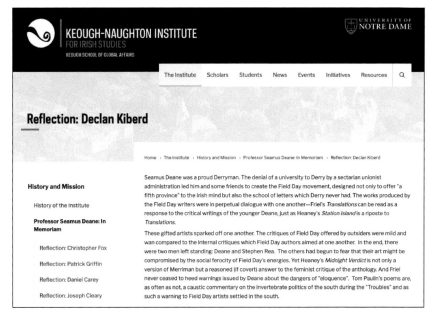

Upon Seamus Deane's death in 2021, the critic Declan Kiberd recalled that the Field Day movement had been established as a 'School of Letters' for Derry, after its denial of a university by a 'sectarian unionist administration'.

He noted the School of Health Sciences was one of the university's largest and his intervention reminded the Economy Department that it held the purse strings.

"Higher education policy for allied health sits with the Department of Health and not this Department, however this Department allocates funding for these courses through the core grant allocation, on the basis of Health advice," Mr Lyons said, in what some people viewed as a warning.

The Northern Ireland Civil Service's attitude towards Magee has also come under the microscope.

A Freedom of Information request submitted to the department revealed that civil servants wrote to the Minister and her Special Advisor on 28 April 2020 – a month after the letter from Mr Lyons.

In what was branded an "anti-Derry attack sheet" by the Derry University Group, they outlined their expert view that Magee expansion would cost £300m in capital with recurrent funding in excess of £100m needed.

An outline business case highlighted a preferred option of expansion to 9,400 Full Time Equivalents (FTEs), including provision of an additional 2,636 full time undergraduate places at Ulster University's Magee campus and 750 additional students delivered via the North West Regional College by 2025.

Under the sub-heading 'Broader Magee Expansion', the civil servants questioned whether there was any need for more students in Northern Ireland.

They said analysis by their Higher Education Division had determined there was a net under-supply of graduates of just 585 per annum.

They went on to question the "high level of uncertainty of the capital costs included in the high level Plan".

They also cited "the lack of any information on the demand from/appetite from students of filling places at the Magee site" (a fact seemingly debunked by Ulster University itself, who said demand for health courses "outstrips available places many times over").

They were worried about the "potential for displacement effects on Queen's University and UU's other sites in Coleraine and Jordanstown", raising:

- The lack of sufficient detail regarding the purported economic benefits of the proposal;

- The lack of information on alternative options if there were to be an expansion in places, and the contrasting benefits from such options if the expansion were to take place in these alternative locations, and

The people of Derry were outraged at Stormont's decision to refuse the city a university. (Pictures courtesy of the Derry Journal).

- The funding implications of any proposed expansion and its repercussive effects on all of higher education provision.

Pointing the finger at Ulster University, DfE then said: "UU was clear that it would not and could not progress expansion at Magee until a decision was made by government to provide (either by increasing student fees or increasing the teaching grant provided per student) additional recurrent funding to address the deficit between what universities receive in Northern Ireland and what universities receive in England for all undergraduate places.

"This precondition from UU meant that the case could never proceed in advance of any such decision being taken by the Executive."

The department had written to UU in February 2019 encouraging the university to review its plans for Magee.

Amongst its advice was questioning "the rationale for locating additional higher education places in the Magee Campus, as opposed to other geographical locations with further and more detailed explanation in relation to sub-regional economic benefits".

The 'attack sheet' concluded: "The former Vice-Chancellor, Paddy Nixon, wrote back to the Department in September 2019 stating that whilst the university remains committed to securing expansion of its Magee campus, the case was not commissioned by the University, and it did not consider wider strategic matters of importance to the institution and cannot be viewed in isolation from wider University priorities.

"The University notes that the business case requires updating prior to any consideration by the Department or Executive which it would provide in due course.

"Through the course of our engagement on the University's Greater Belfast Development project, it is clear that any expansion in the North West would be impossible without significant additional grant.

"It is possible that the university will think carefully around the risks involved in it committing to another very large scale and complex capital project, which although there is no clarity on costs, is likely to run into many hundreds of millions of pounds all of which would be sought as a grant from government. UU's recently stated position is that it will also be required to review the reasonableness around the numbers of any forecast expansion in relation to need and demand."

PART VII
So what has changed?

Table 19.1 Demographic and socio-economic data for potential locations for new universities.

	Sub-regional economic strengths	Median age of population in years, 2017	Job density*	% of 16-64 population with Level 4 qualifications or higher, 2017	% of 16+ population in employment in professional and managerial jobs, 2017**
Barnstaple, North Devon	Pharmaceuticals, agriculture	47.1	1.05	37.7%	43.5%
Berwick-upon-Tweed (Northumberland data)	Leisure, farming, forestry, fishing	47.7	0.65	35.0%	40.4%
Chesterfield	Specialist metals, light engineering, IT	44.3	0.81	26.1%	32.4%
Derry-Londonderry	Biotechnology, textiles, creative industries, agriculture	37.2	0.57	22.0%	30.7%
Doncaster	Engineering	41.4	0.72	23.6%	34.5%
Grimsby (NE Lincolnshire data)	Maritime industries, marine biology	44.0	0.79	22.0%	32.9%
Peterborough	Intensive agriculture, biotechnology, light engineering	36.2	1.03	25.6%	37.3%
Shrewsbury	Agriculture, defence	46.7	0.80	36.9	40.2
Southend	Leisure, financial services, light engineering, IT	41.5	0.70	30.7%	46.9%
Wigan	Food and drink, glass, leisure	42.2	0.59	26.8%	34.7%
UK		40.1	0.84 (GB)	38.6% (GB)	45.7% (GB)

*Jobs to total 16-64 population.
**Standard Occupational Classification codes 1-3.
Sources: Annual Population Survey, ONS business data.

Statistics published by the British government's Levelling Up Group in 2022, showing Derry's massive disadvantage.

As former *Derry Journal* editor Frank Curran noted in his 1986 book, *Derry: Countdown to Disaster*, extreme unionism didn't want a university going to Derry because it would render the gerrymander virtually impossible and make unchallenged unionist control of the North less certain.

'Extreme unionism', to use Curran's term, still opposes university expansion in Derry but often couches this in softer tones, by insisting on delivery for Coleraine as well. On the surface, liberal unionist politicians are today nominally supportive of Magee expansion.

While the old unionist supremacy is long gone, there are still Ministers and indeed civil servants who argue there is no need for any significant investment in the North West. They frame Northern Ireland as a one city-region. Antrim/Belfast is the one-stop-shop with the best infrastructure, 83% of students and therefore skilled labour, a higher percentage of civil servants now than it had ten years ago, with dominance in the financial and insurance, as well as the information and communication sectors, as well as the food, beverages, textiles and clothing sectors.

It boasts the best infrastructure, and hoovers up at least 80% of arts funding to boot.

But, once they see attempts to restore regional balance, such as happened when Diane Dodds was Economy Minister, they flex their power and remind supposedly-autonomous institutions just who holds the purse.

There is a particular issue with Derry, a fear of acknowledging the elephant in the room; a fear of acknowledging the enormity of the injustice that was done to this city-region and is still being done.

In 2024, the new Economy Minister Conor Murphy himself came to Derry to announce a taskforce for Magee expansion to 10,000 students.

While here, he spoke of the Executive coming together to agree a £150m funding package for the Strule Shared Education Campus in Omagh. Why over recent years could similar capital investment not have been committed to Magee?

I'm no oracle but let me hazard a guess. A shared education campus is seen as less 'controversial'. Just as pumping billions of pounds into Belfast is more acceptable because there is a more even split between Catholics and Protestants. It keeps everyone happy; it is politically expedient.

Because once Derry is mentioned, ears prick up. Why should Derry get that? What about Coleraine?

Historically, and it continues to today, Derry cannot get support without Coleraine getting the same.

That is evidenced with the university issue. Ulster University invests around £7m directly in Magee (I'm saying directly as they like to talk of vague university-wide investment) over the past decade. And the same amount goes to Coleraine.

The Economy Department invests around £18m in Magee. The same goes to Coleraine.

Therefore, both areas got approximately £25m direct capital investment from DfE and UU.

FURTHER EDUCATION DEFICIT

Derry is the second city in the North. It is at least three times bigger than Coleraine – and the biggest UK city with a European land border.

If the economic principle applies that Belfast gets more than Derry because of its heft, why does it not apply when we are looking at Derry and Coleraine?

Is it a hangover for the Troubles? Is it that those 'troublemakers' in Derry who essentially dismantled unionist hegemony should be starved of investment? Is it simply because of the geography, as some claim, because our neighbours in Donegal (which incidentally doesn't have a city the size of Derry) are also neglected by the Irish Government?

Food for thought. I'll let the reader draw their own conclusions.

Because here's the thing. Although Coleraine and Derry were treated equally in terms of higher education funding over the past ten years, they weren't when it came to further education funding.

You guessed it. Derry wasn't the beneficiary.

The second city received £16.5m which was split between two campuses in the city while the seaside town got £40m for a new campus.

Taken in the round, that means Coleraine, a town one quarter the size of Derry City, got £65m from Stormont's Economy Department and Derry got approximately £41.5m.

Coleraine's partner college in the Northern Regional College (NRC) area, the small town of Ballymena, was also awarded £45m for a new campus.

NRC also got £13.1m for minor capital works.

Armagh got £34.78m for a new campus and Enniskillen got £31m.

Therefore places with a fraction of Derry's population and without their own universities got more or close to the same level of FE investment as the second city got for HE and FE combined.

Now, let's turn to our close neighbours in Strabane, an area which has suffered terribly when it comes to disinvestment.

Census figures show that Strabane has a population of 13,507. Coleraine (24,483), Ballymena (31,205), Armagh (16,000) and Enniskillen (14,000).

Strabane is the only town in Northern Ireland which is having to use City Deal money from the British Government in order to expand its FE College campus. Why? Again, this is money which should be invested directly by Stormont.

Strabane got a measly £53k from the Economy Department. Armagh and Enniskillen are of comparable size yet they got 656 times more and 585 times more respectively.

Now, we get sensible socks who hide their bigotry behind intellectual language at times. Or say it is simply impossible to deliver regional equality.

Why so? Belfast can surely be the economic driver in the East, which it is thanks to decades of disproportionate funding.

TRICKLE-DOWN MYTH

By the same token, Derry can be the main economic driver for the West. It's quite simple really. Most areas west of the Bann do not benefit from Belfast-centrism. Trickle-down economics is a myth.

Others say Belfast is too close to Derry, there's no need for another city with a sizeable university.

Limerick with about 30,000 students is closer to Galway with circa 26,000 students and Cork with over 34,000 students. Why can it be done in the Republic and not NI?

Glasgow with over 92,000 students is closer to Edinburgh with 76,000 students.

Manchester with 84,000 students is closer to Liverpool with 64,000 students.

The list could go on in other parts of these islands.

Yet, there is a deeply-embedded mindset in the Northern Ireland Civil Service, and it has to be said, in wider society, that Belfast should be the exception to the rule.

In short, it's a nonsense argument to conceal inherent biases.

So when people emerge to say it is about geography or Northern Ireland being too small or because Derry is not big enough.

Remember this: Belfast supremacy, eastern dominance, did not happen by accident. It did not happen overnight. This has been manufactured and is decades in the making.

From the insistence on pushing ahead with the creation of Craigavon, diverting money away from large-scale development in Derry in the mid-1960s, to funnelling money into Belfast under power-sharing, Derry's place as the second city in the North has been undermined.

It has been systematically downgraded to the point where cities with thriving universities like Limerick and Galway are bypassing it in terms of population size.

If that situation is not reversed, and fast, the city will experience further decline.

Outdated university targets can no longer be allowed to stand. It is about ambition. About looking to the likes of Galway and Limerick for inspiration and believing we're every bit as deserving as them.

Derry is not asking for the moon and the stars. We are demanding equality.

NEW THINKING FROM ROYAL IRISH ACADEMY

Following the Royal Irish Academy report in 2021, the Irish government contributed £38m to develop the Magee campus.

In 2021, researchers from the Royal Irish Academy Higher Education Futures Taskforce explored the role of regions and place in higher education across the island of Ireland. Their aim was to develop a viable vision for higher education on the island of Ireland up to 2035, taking into account major global and local changes such as Brexit and increasing North-South collaboration in education.

The RIA highlighted the anomalous situation of Northern Ireland being **the only region in these islands which was devoid of any independent oversight of its tertiary education provision.**

It said there would be merit in developing a **more transparent funding model** to allow meaningful comparisons with UK institutions and between institutions and campuses in Northern Ireland.

The Academy recommended the creation of a **NI tertiary education oversight body** to advise government, help define sectoral mission and ensure greater coordination and regional distribution within the university and FE sectors.

The Taskforce also particularly identified a **need to address HE under-provision in the North West as a matter of urgency.**

The researchers concluded that "without a cross-border planning model based on all of the institutions and campuses of FE and HE provision in the northwest region, and whose primary focus is its enhancement based on needs and opportunities independent of the priorities of the capital cities in both jurisdictions, the North West cannot attain its full potential in a sustainable way".

In other words, a successful NWU can only thrive if it is allowed to be autonomous of Belfast.

This accords with a case study example outlined in the recent statement by the Secretary of State for Northern Ireland, citing the potential of a cross-

> The Taskforce recommends the creation of a NI tertiary education oversight body to advise government, help define sectoral mission and ensure greater co-ordination and regional distribution within the university and FE sectors. Given the critical nature of tertiary education in determining the economic, social and cultural welfare of NI, the establishment of such a body warrants high priority within the NI Executive's agenda. While recognising the significance of the proposal to establish a NI Skills Council, it is not believed that such a council, in the absence of a dedicated tertiary education oversight body, would have the specificity or focus to establish greater co-ordination, regional distribution, resource distribution and oversight within and between the HE and FE sectors across all of Northern Ireland. Such an oversight body could also provide informed input to an all-island co-ordination of tertiary education and research and help ensure that Northern Ireland's tertiary education system is appropriately placed to deliver the economic, social and cultural needs of the region to optimal effect.

The RIA's 2021 report first raised the need for an oversight commission for higher education in the North.

The RIA's 2021 report led to calls for a new North-South body for cross-border university development in the North West.

border university to address historic under-investment in the northwest region in accordance with the UK government's 'levelling up' agenda.

For the first time in a century, the direction of travel was slowly but surely starting to shift away from Belfast, which was now overheating, towards Derry.

In 2023, the Irish government, through its Shared Island Unit, announced a €44m grant for a new teaching and student-services building at Magee, in a bid to boost numbers at the campus.

TRANSFORMING A 'LAGGING REGION'

The Shared Island Unit also funded a new Royal Irish Academy report specifically into university provision on both sides of the border in the North West – which the EU has categorised as a 'lagging region', (72% of the EU GDP per capita, down from 82% in five years).

Published in April 2024, this report recommended 'affirmative action' to redress the brain drain, low levels of participation in HE and regional imbalance in the North West, by establishing an independent cross-border North West University, stretching from Coleraine to Mayo with Derry as the central hub.

The new institute would sustain a new North West economic corridor and would be jointly funded by the Northern Ireland/Westminster and RoI governments, each funding activities within their respective jurisdictions.

The report's authors – Gerry McKenna, Jennifer Kenneally and Sinéad Riordan – stressed that the 'spatial distribution' of student places was a 'political imperative…an essential and integral part of regional planning, not determined by the limitations or competing priorities of individual institutions'.

Economic consultant John Daly, who advised the report, said 'regional autonomy was the key to the report's implementation. He recommended: more investment in higher and further education in the region; building on the existing strengths (and campuses) of the North West; regional incentives for students (such as grants and/or fee decreases); and greater collaboration between education bodies.

The Academy also, again, underlined the need for independent scrutiny of the North's university sector – citing the massive regional imbalance in students. And this proposal has since been backed by Derry & Strabane District Council.

The Academy's proposals dovetailed with Dublin's Project Ireland 2040 plan, the national planning framework to ensure Ireland's economic, environmental and social future.

Sligo is already a regional growth centre under the plan, and representatives North and South are arguing that Derry, as a cross-border regional hub, must now be included as the major regional centre of the North West in the strategy.

'IT WILL HAPPEN'

Veteran campaigner Conal McFeely says there needs to be much more urgency and determination from the political sector in the North West to deliver the university.

'Our new leaders have become conditioned by Belfast and London politicians and civil servants to accept crumbs from the table – or they will get nothing at all,' he said.

"They need to wake up to what is happening around them – and the fact that their region has been downgraded and depleted and sacrificed at the altar of the Belfast Agenda. They need to remember why John Hume saw the university as so important – it is the centre of this city's recovery and its social and economic regeneration.

"In the meantime, promise after promise has led to taskforce after taskforce and delay after delay. And all the money goes out the back door from Stormont into Belfast. The statistics – as Garrett Hargan has so expertly brought to light – do not lie.

"The failure to let Derry run its own university today is a political decision taken to service Belfast and stifle Derry – just as it was in the 1960s. It is about social control by the state – to quote Lord Adonis, a 'long-running social and sectarian scandal'. There is no other part of the world where this would be tolerated.

"It has taken fresh, outside voices, from both Dublin – in the form of the Royal Irish Academy – and London in the form of the British Labour Party to put this issue back at the centre of the educational, and civil rights, agenda. And we intend to keep it there until we have a fully-independent, community-focussed, cross-border university in the North West, with Derry at its core.

Veteran campaigner Conal McFeely at the Derry University Group's 55-foot long 'Wall of Protest' on the Strand Road, erected in 2022.

"Stormont, as a matter of priority, needs to appoint a Universities Oversight Commission, such as exists in the form of the Higher Education Authority in the South, to supervise and regulate the sector. The simple argument for it being, can you imagine any scrutiny body allowing 83% of students and 93% of capital spend to be restricted to one overheated city?

"The new North West university is going to happen – no doubt about it. We will encourage Dublin and London to keep it as their top priority on its East-West, British-Irish Intergovernmental council until it is up and running. The Irish have already shown us their commitment, and we have little doubt – given their massive good work in developing Higher Education across the island and their determination to develop the North West as a prosperous city-region – that they will make good on their promises to us. There are very promising signs too from the incoming British government, who have recognised the importance of this issue while in opposition.

"This, after so many decades, is Derry's opportunity. It is vital that we seize it."

'COMMUNITIES NEED TO MAKE MORE NOISE'

"It is ludicrous that we need to continue to 'make a case for the University' – that case was made 60 years ago and is well known in the corridors of power. Arguably, however, this case is less well known or understood within our communities – and we need more noise coming from everyone in our communities to get this over the line. Our politicians will only put pressure on the civil service and make this happen in response to continuous and vocal demands from the electorate.

"The challenge with any campaign at a time like this is that politicians are so easily able to deflect and divide the general public with cries of 'No money in the budget' or 'There are more important issues requiring public focus and resources at the moment.' We have heard these excuses for 60 years – whilst the North West has steadily declined.

"The problem is that many people do not see the relevance or the connection between the University and *their* daily lives and the key issues affecting *them*, particularly those for whom attending university was traditionally not an option. However they *are* intrinsicly linked.

"The single biggest, most effective economic lever at our disposal in terms of regenerating the North West is the development of appropriate higher and third-level education provision. This move addresses a number of the key structural problems which face / affect our region (and communities):

• Providing more opportunities and removing financial and logistical barriers for young people from the most disadvantaged communities – by allowing them to access education in their own town (reducing accommodation/living/travel costs).

• Enhanced provision on our doorstep may be the decisive factor in encouraging a first generation of new Third-level students (from more disadvantaged backgrounds), encouraging those who may otherwise decide not to attend university to do so. This enables a step-change in socio-economic mobility and supports the building of generational equity / prosperity.

• Reducing brain drain – giving those who would otherwise attend university in another city, region or country the opportunity to stay in their own town – building regional capacity and competitiveness.

• Providing opportunities for those looking to return to education in later life who may have family commitments, caring duties or similarly enable those of varying abilities or health limitations to access education in an environment with more localised (family) supports.

• Better skills provision for the local economy means the region is more attractive to potential employers – attracting inward investment (which means more and better paid jobs).

• Enhanced provision means greater indigenous creativity and enterprise which helps build sustainable jobs and social capital.

• More students means more money spent and circulating in the local economy (favouring local businesses and workers over the long-run).

• More money in the local economy means more money in the system to fund other vital public services to meet community needs.

• A new university (with appropriate support infrastructure and services) will enhance the physical environment and contribute to the overall socio-economic wellbeing and cultural diversity of the region.

• Ultimately many of the issues affecting the North West are the result of generational disadvantage and poverty (brought on by decades of underinvestment and isolation). If we wish to raise the average income and wage in the North West (which is currently half that of Belfast) – we need a mechanism to inspire hope, incentivise and stimulate greater economic participation, activity and productivity.

A section of the attendees at June 2024's RIA presentation at Ráth Mór, including: Prof. Gerry McKenna, Kevin Hippsley, Joe Martin, Anthony Hutton, Mark Durkan, Conal McFeely, Patrick Duffy, Pat McArt, Cónal Ó Mianáin, Damien McKane, Amie Gallagher, Terry Wright and Catherine Pollock.

"Yes there are logistical issues which must be overcome – but with an open mind and some creative solutions we can unlock even greater benefits for the region. An example of this type of approach is the potential multi-campus decentralised model, embedded in our communities, as visualised by the students of Edinburgh University School of Architecture. This approach integrates communities with the university at a local level and addresses the current more 'detached' system, which may appear to only benefit communities on a 'trickle-down' basis. A properly-inetgrated university catalyses community activity and spearheads social change, creating benefits from the ground up.

"If we are serious about addressing these key structural issues holding back economic development and prosperity in the North West, there is only one viable, achievable way to do this – and we would argue that an independent cross-border model (which retains the ability to access European and cross-jursidictional funding) is the ideal mechanism to deliver this change.

"Yes there are major issues facing families and communities in the North West – and our political elite will say that we need to prioritise one demand over the other ('there simply is not enough to go around'). That does not seem to ever be the case for Belfast however – who get what they want/ need whenever it suits them. There is an old saying, which everyone is very familiar with in this part of the world – 'whoever cries the loudest…' Well the North West has been silenced for too long, we need to find our voice again, our communities need to make more noise – we need both governments and our executive to stand up, listen and finally deliver."

EPILOGUE
Hume's vision still resonates
By Pat McArt

University for Derry chair John Hume, Mayor Albert Anderson and Eddie McAteer MP, leading the 25000-strong cavalcade from the North West to Stormont in 1965. (Picture courtesy Derry Journal).

In the early 1960s when the government at Stormont made clear that with Queen's University operating at full capacity a second university outside of Belfast was to be given the go-ahead a then unknown local school-teacher, John Hume, and some others, formed a University for Derry Committee.

With Hume as chairman, they led the charge in advocating for the siting of this multi-million pound project for their city.

Local media reports from this time make it clear that with the small third-level Magee College already operating – and with both nationalist and unionists locally joining in the campaign – they believed they had such a cast-iron case that not even the Unionist regime at Stormont could deny them.

They were wrong.

There was no 'second university for the second city'; it was awarded to the small market town of Coleraine.

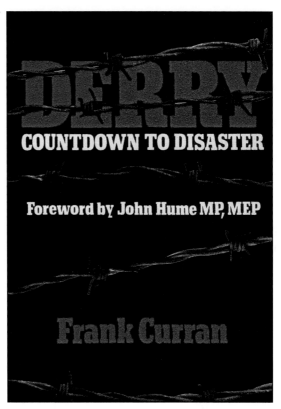

The deliberate denial of a university to Derry in the 1960s – and how it happened – looms large in former Derry Journal editor Frank Curran's 1986 history of the NI Civil Rights Movement.

That decision, many old timers in Derry still insist, was the spark for the Troubles which were to erupt in the city just a couple of years later.

In fact, it's a decision that still rankles deeply to this day.

In the spring of 2024, the latest episode in this long running 'University for Derry' saga took a significant twist when the experts from the Royal Irish Academy's Education Futures Taskforce published an Irish government-commissioned report which suggested that an 'ambitious' federal cross-border third-level institution should merit 'serious consideration'.

That option has gone down particularly well in the city, something the Derry University Group (DUG) has been pushing for a very long time.

This lobby grouping wants an independent university free of Ulster University (UU) control. Put simply, there is history here – they no longer have any faith in what they consider a Belfast-centric organisation to deliver for Derry. The UU, of course, will hotly dispute this.

The DUG has been scathing about UUs commitment to Derry, suggesting it has 'a long trail of broken promises and unfilled commitments'.

Campaigners frequently point to the fact that more than 80% of Northern Ireland's third level students are based in Belfast. And to the fact 95% of the capital spend is also allocated there. This is not matched anywhere else in either Britain or Ireland.

It is, quite literally, worth billions annually to the greater Belfast economy.

They also point to "how Cork, Tralee, Limerick, Galway, Westport, Sligo and Letterkenny have been transformed economically" in recent decades by higher education provision.

Derry, meanwhile, they maintain, lags in the doldrums.

The RIA report largely supports this assessment.

The report noted: "(There is) a general acceptance that the northwest region of the island of Ireland has been disadvantaged in both jurisdictions due to inevitable limitations imposed by a land border and its peripherality from the major centres of political and economic power and focus, namely Belfast and Dublin', the 'relative lack of investment...evident in limited transport systems (road, rail and air) and in inadequate broadband and other communication facilities."

Jeremy Corbyn meeting university campaigner Pat McArt (centre), during the former Labour leader's visit to the North West in 2022. Included are Alison Stoecker, Barry James and Laura Alvarez.

McAteer saw Lemass as 'naive', says Derry book

AFTER YEARS of travelling to Dublin to brief Ministers about the plight of Northern Nationalists under the old Stormont Government, Mr Eddie McAteer recalled: "I got hospitality but little real support."

Frank Curran is a former editor of the Derry Journal. Describing Mr McAteer's view of southern politicians he says that the former Nationalist Party leader, who died last March, "felt that partition had eroded their nationalism." Mr McAteer felt that there was no comprehension of the Northern problem in the Republic and that politicians did not appreciate the disabilities under which the nationalist people lived.

Mr Curran, a close friend of Mr McAteer, interviewed him while researching his book, "Derry — Countdown to Disaster" (Gill & MacMillan) which was launched officially in Derry last month. It is an account of the major events in the city, and the politicians involved in them, which led to the outbreak of the present troubles in the North in 1968.

A new book about the injustices in Derry which formed the background to the outbreak of the present troubles has been published. MARTIN COWLEY spoke to the author, Derry journalist Frank Curran. 1/11/86

Mr Curran details in particular the Unionist gerrymander of Derry which ensured that until 1969, 11,000 Unionist voters had 12 corporation seats, while 19,000 nationalist voters had only eight. But one of the major reasons for the wave of anti-Stormont feeling was the decision in 1965 by the Terence O'Neill Government to site second university in Coleraine instead of in Derry city. The decision was carried through in spite of a united demand by both Protestants and Catholics in Derry, 25,000 of whom travelled to Stormont in a cavalcade of cars to press the city's claim for the university. The Stormont vote on the university question took place in February, 1965, one month after the historic Lemass-O'Neill talks at Stormont.

In his book Mr Curran writes that until nationalists projected the view for Unionist consumption that Dublin automatically sympathised and sided with them. This bolstered Catholic morale and acted as a deterrent to possible further Unionist excesses. Mr Curran commented: "In fact this Dublin 'guarantee' of Northern minority rights was no guarantee at all. It was a myth, pure and simple."

An example of the brittleness of the facade was given to him by Mr McAteer who recalled a meeting which he had with the Taoiseach, Mr Sean Lemass, shortly after the Lemass-O'Neill talks. Mr McAteer said that when he met Lemass he received "neither the encouragement nor understanding of our position that I expected." Lemass said that he felt the Catholics were just as intractable as the Protestants.

"It was hardly the reaction I expected from a Taoiseach with his Republican background to the representative of the oppressed Irish minority in the Six Counties," Mr McAteer said.

He though Lemass was "naive" to believe that Unionists could be wooed towards a united Ireland through industrial progress in the Republic. "I came away with the conviction that as far as Sean Lemass was concerned, the Northern Irish were very much on their own," Mr McAteer said.

Mr Curran remarked that although Dublin and London were now heavily involved in the Northern problem, 20 years ago they "couldn't care less." The brutality which the RUC displayed during the banned October 5th march in Derry in 1968 had been displayed in similar fashion in 1949, 1951 and 1952, when nationalists, including Mr McAteer, tried to march through their own city, Mr Curran said. At the time over 30 years ago it was treated as a "one-day wonder" big story in the Dublin papers but nobody there thought to ask the question why it happened.

On the university issue Mr Curran commented: "Eddie and John Hume both felt that the university was the point of no return. Eddie described it as 'the point of despair.' For Eddie it meant that all the parliamentary work of years had been proved to be useless. For Hume it meant that Stormont had to be challenged, possibly on the streets. For Derry it meant that the last chance of real community unity had been lost."

Frank Curran tells Irish Times reporter Martin Cowley that the refusal to grant Derry a university marked a turning point in John Hume's life.

I have first-hand knowledge of both places. While I spent most of my adult life in Derry, I grew up in Letterkenny in the 1970's. It was little more than a backwater town then, a place where the weekly cattle mart was the highlight of commercial activity. So, when the Regional Technical College opened it was like the parting of the Red Sea – the UK textile giant Courtaulds located a big plant in the town, new shops opened, housing estates were built, and the satellite villages suddenly had influxes of people seeking accommodation.

It has made a big difference to the town, but a couple of significant indicators of economic inequality remain not least that Derry has the least disposable income in the North whilst Donegal has the least in the Republic.

Another thing this region has in common is that today the Atlantic Technical University has in the region of 4,000 plus full-time students whilst Magee, despite that 60 year campaign for a full-sized university, has a little over 5,000 full-time and part-time combined. Galway, Limerick and Cork have institutions with four/five times these student numbers.

Back in the 1960's when the university for Derry campaign kicked off The Kinks had a big hit with 'Tired of Waiting'. In 2024 the people here are way beyond tired of waiting.

Hume's vision still resonates. His belief in the power of education to transform communities and bridge divides hasn't gone away.

• *Pat McArt was Managing Editor of the Derry Journal from 1981 to 2006.*

University of Edinburgh School of Architecture and Landscape Architecture –
reimaging a new vision for a new university.

APPENDIX I
The University Of Daire

Reflections and possibilities from the University of Edinburgh
School of Architecture and Landscape Architecture

The MSc in Architectural and Urban Design (AUD) is a one-year postgraduate Master's programme that provides specialist training in urban design for candidates who already hold an architectural degree. In the AUD studio, we develop design proposals for specific international urban conditions, focusing on the contribution of design to the broader life and workings of the city. Research methods involve intense fieldwork in the chosen city of study, sharpening and extending skills in developing contemporary urban contexts through analysis, research, and experimentation.

Since 2022, we have been studying the ecosophic, linguistic, precolonial, and transborder landscapes of Doire/Daire/Derry (meaning the Oak Grove) for meaning and for the possibilities of a New University. This studio runs parallel to and complements the ongoing efforts of the 'Derry University Group,' a local group advocating for an independent, cross-border university in Derry. This initiative sustains the call made by civil rights movement leader, teacher, and architect of the Northern Ireland peace process, John Hume, in 1963.

Course Organisers: Dr. Killian O Dochartaigh Dr. Dorian Wiszniewski

Course Tutors: Dr. Dorian Wiszniewski, Dr. Killian O Dochartaigh, Neil Cunning, Paul Pattinson, Leo Xian, Mark Hilley, En Fang, and Ruta Turcinaviciute

Students 2022-2024: Lena Bozhko, Tianxiao Chai, Ziyao Chen, Aden Chen, Qiuyu Chen, Kaite Chen, Weitian Chen, Yuxuan Chen, Rumman Chowdhury, Yunshang Fang, Dandan Feng, Yiqing Feng, Shaowen Hao, Jiachen Hu, Zhong Hui, Min Huang, Ruoxue Huang, Xiaoyu Jian, Mengni Jiang, Bao Jia, Jiahui Ji, Ang Li, Qian Li, Tianrui Li, Xinyue Li, Wenli Liao, Yingchun Liao, Su Liu, Yinuo Liu, Yian Luan, Jiaheng Lyu, Yixiao Mao, Shayne Ni, Qian Ran, Haotian Ren, Jie Sheng, Jessie Shu, Sruthi Suresh Babu, Ao Sun, Yuran Tang, Junxi Tao, Vysakh Veluthedath Pankajakshan, Peilin Yang, Chen Yang, Peng Yang, Yuyin Xiao, Yifan Xia, Xinyi Xu, Elias Zhang, Yu Zhang, Yutong Zhang, Ziyu Zhang, Zongwei Zhang, Chusheng Zheng, Beiying Zhu, Meng Yuan, Kai Wu, Xiaowen Wu, and Yihan Wang.

University of Edinburgh students and faculty on a study visit to Derry in 2022.

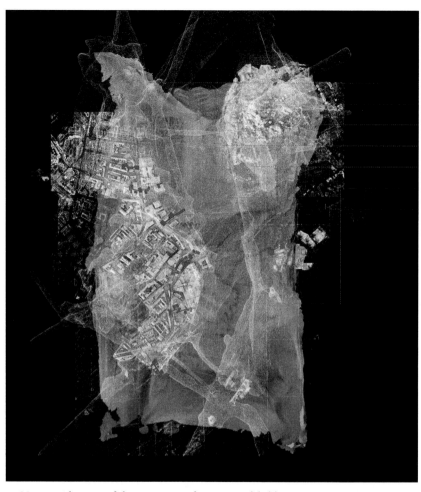

New visualization of the University of Derry, Modeled by Peng Yang, Ang Li, 2022.

Above & below: A visualisation of a Hydroponics Institute located on former Tillie and Henderson Shirt Factory, Images by Peng Yang, 2023.

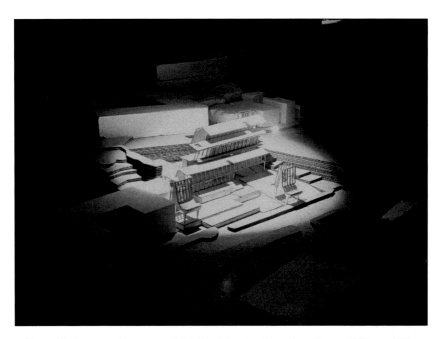

Above: Hydroponics Factory and Student Housing located on former Tillie and Henderson Shirt Factory. Below: Water purification plant on former Tillie and Henderson Shirt Factory, Images by Peng Yang, 2023.

Above & below: Render of landscaped ground below Research Hive for Fish Ecology and Conservation, located on site of former fish market (and Rialto Theatre) by Yuxuan Chen, 2022.

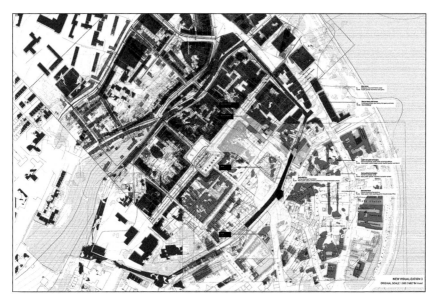

New visualization of one of seven colleges within the University of Derry. Image by Lena Bozhko, Yuxuan Chen, Mengni Jiang, 2022.

Students Lena Bozhko, Yuxuan Chen, Mengni Jiang study the new ecologies within in Prehen quarry, 2023.

Derry University – Right to the City is a Right to the Environment is a Right to Higher Education

Dr. Dorian Wiszniewski

When Patrick Geddes worked with Rabindranath Tagore to help him develop his thoughts and plans for Santiniketan, currently *Visva Bharati University* (a title that states the aspiration for the communion of the world with India) in West Bengal, the vision, much like he articulated later for his *College des Ecossais* in Montpellier in the South of France as the precursor to his "Cite Universitaire" (a series of local and international study centres attached to all the great universities of the world), was for the integration of different disciplines through a nurturing of the landscape. The garden is as much a place of learning as the classroom. Sun, shade, rain and shelter are all considered architecture. However, so is knowledge. The architecture of epistemology is the same consideration as the architecture of a university building. The architecture of epistemology is to be led by a knowledge of the environment. Geddes' triad of place-folk-work operates along-side the urgency to think globally and act locally. These early calls for climate conscious environmentalism suggest that the architecture of outside space and inside space have the same environmental and material-culture specificity. Modernity was not a question of the continuing dominion of man over nature or the domination and securing of privilege of some men over other men. For both Tagore and Geddes, the university was a place to nurture greater relations between humans and non-humans. Why not situate a university in the landscape first? Why not let the architecture and epistemological inclinations be directed at least partially by that landscape, acting through deep understanding of locality but also how this environment can contribute to global epistemology.

Therefore, the starting point for our work on Derry University is the Geddesian inflected study of the "past, present and possible" of Derry. There is no past to Derry University, unless we think back to the time of St. Columb and perhaps even some references to Brehon oral traditions and the wonderful notion of hospitality, which still seems to exist. There is no present to Derry University, except to be reminded of the recurrent presence of its absence and the reminders of its absence that we come partly to understand by the return of some of its citizens who have studied elsewhere, some citizens who have remained whilst ruing their lost opportunities and of some citizens who are not yet aware of the full potential for their city by these absent opportunities. However, Derry University is certainly possible. Therefore, rather than being further restrained by the politics of Derry history, we choose to look at Derry first through the lens of its beautiful landscape. We see it as another Santiniketan. It is a place that works with its seasons and the palpable presence of its landscape, both thick and thin places. It is a beautifully wet place. However, the history of its wetness has been paralleled by a history of disdain for the wetness coupled with the history of enclosures with concomitant privilege given to some whilst others are deliberately cast into the mire. We begin the project of Derry by raising the virtues whilst addressing some of the uneasy aspects of wetness. We keep in mind Geddes, commonly referred to as the father of Town Planning, and his *Notations of Life* model which states quite clearly that a town needs a university as the means for it to be a city and properly look after its folk.

Dr. Dorian Wiszniewski
Senior Lecturer
Architectural and Urban Design, Theory and Criticism
Programme Director: PhD Architecture By Design; MSc Architectural and Urban Design
Edinburgh School of Architecture and Landscape Architecture
Edinburgh College of Art
University of Edinburgh

Staying with Trouble in Place: Derry University as an Agent for Political and Social Change[1]

Dr. Killian O'Dochartaigh

Born in Derry, I am a subject of a post-colonial, post-conflict state. As an architect and educator, I am interested in how architecture contributes to the making and unmaking of troubled places. More precisely, I am interested in how architecture – as a discipline of standardised knowledge and practices – extends the colonial state and yet can also be used to construct a 'shared future.' This conflicted view of architecture emerges from my experience of living and practising within the post-conflict redevelopment of Sierra Leone, Liberia, and Rwanda over the past 14 years.

In 2009, I was based in Rwanda to oversee the construction of a community centre designed for a local NGO serving an under-resourced community in the capital, Kigali. This centre and NGO used football as a medium to discuss ethnic intolerance between Tutsi and Hutu youth. This development was one of many commissions by European and American architects contributing to the post-conflict reconstruction of Rwanda following the 1994 Genocide.

That year, along with several East African architects, we established the first school of architecture on the remains of the city's colonial plan and infrastructure of a military camp. Located in small buildings next to where ten Belgian peacekeepers were shot in 1994, we began to train the first cohort of Rwandan architects. Despite lacking textbooks, furniture, or drawing boards, we taught foundational design studios in architecture, urban planning, participatory design, ecology, and core seminars in drawing, model making, architectural history, and theory.

What became apparent, however, was that the new built environment of Rwanda, being reconstructed around us, did not emerge from the place-based specifics or lived realities of the majority. Instead, it emulated the trend for high-modernist, utopian urban visions often favoured by new political

1 Part of this title is borrowed from Donna' J.Haraway. See Haraway, Donna J. "Staying with the Trouble: Making Kin in the Chthulucene." Durham [N.C.]: Duke University Press, 2016. https://doi.org/10.1515/9780822373780.

regimes. In Africa, these visions are particularly violent as they rapaciously destroy everyday life, dispossessing the urban poor, subsistence farmers, and indigenous groups, and eradicating their vernacular building, settlement, and livelihood practices. To destroy the vernacular, whether a language or architectural practice, is to create a homogenous, sanitised, controlled, dehumanised, and disassociated place – a non-place without identity and substantive meaning.

In observing this, we re-oriented the curriculum and our pedagogical methods to have the students to constructively engage with, critique, and respond to this strange, deeply unjust emergent built environment. Our pedagogies were event-based, embraced site-specific methods, and echoed grassroots activism and adult education in the Global South in the 1970s.[2] These methods involved students to participate and embed themselves with the real world, to question authority and empower them to shape their own future. Over the next three years, our students engaged with architecture not simply as a design tool, but as an active agent in shaping political and social change in Rwanda Continuing this architectural project, I returned home to Derry in 2022, bringing the 'University of Derry' into the studios of the MSc AUD Programme here at ESALA, taught with Dr. Dorian Wiszniewski.

Dr. Killian O'Dochartaigh
Lecturer in Architecture and Urbanism
Co-coordinator of MSc Architectural and Urban Design
Edinburgh School of Architecture and Landscape Architecture
Edinburgh College of Art
University of Edinburgh

2 Freire, Paulo. Pedagogy of the Oppressed. New York: Seabury Press, 1968.

APPENDIX II
Timeline: significant events in the campaign for a Derry University

6th Century AD – A monastic settlement and centre of learning is founded by Colmcille (Columb) on the banks of the Foyle. The settlement would become known as Doire (Derry), the Irish word for oak grove.

1164 – The Teampall Mór, which would serve as Derry's cathedral for more than 300 years, is built close to the site of the original Columban monastery, becoming the official episcopal seat in 1254.

1633 – The first non-Roman Catholic cathedral in Western Europe, St Columb's, is consecrated on the site of the old Teampall Mór (destroyed in 1568).

1865 – Magee College opens, primarily as a Presbyterian theological college, to service the 'social and intellectual advancement of Derry'. It is named after its benefactress Martha Magee.

1880 – Magee becomes a constituent college of the Royal University of Ireland (RUI), allowing students, including women, to complete recognised degrees.

1906 – On the dissolution of the RUI, Magee becomes an autonomous university, with students completing their degrees at Trinity College Dublin.

1940s – Allied Command establishes a massive underground bunker at Magee, from where the Battle of the Atlantic is coordinated.

1963 – To meet the growing demand for higher education, Derry Corporation publishes its manifesto to build a full university at Magee.

1964 The Lockwood Committee is convinced by senior unionists and civil servants to recommend a new university for Coleraine and to close Magee.

1965 – University for Derry chair John Hume leads a cavalcade of 25000 citizens from the North West to Stormont, but the unionist government ratifies the Lockwood Report.

1968 – Hume would link the birth of the civil rights movement to Stormont's decision to refuse Derry its own university.

1969 – The New University of Ulster (NUU) opens outside Coleraine. Magee is retained as a small Institute of Continuing Education, reducing to half its size, but is not allowed to offer undergraduate courses.

1982 – Westminster (UK Government) orders the merger of NUU and the Ulster Polytechnic, to become Ulster University (UU). The merger took place in 1984 and saw a spurt of growth at Magee in the late 1980s/1990s and the return of undergraduate degrees to the campus.

1993 – The International Conflict Research institute (Incore), co-sponsored by the United Nations, is established at Magee.

1993 – UU announces plans for a new £70m Belfast campus at Springvale, ultimately spending £10m before the project collapses.

1995 – On his post-ceasefire visit to Ireland, the US President Bill Clinton inaugurates the Tip O'Neill Chair in Peace Studies (later the Hume-O'Neill Chair) at Incore, Magee.

2001 – Northern Ireland Science Park established. Agreement reached that it should have a base at Magee.

2001 – Academy for Irish Cultural Heritages established at Magee

2003 – Following a long and sustained community campaign, UU announces plans for a new medical school for Magee. It finally opens, after the direct intervention of the two governments, 18 years later, with Derry/Strabane Council agreeing to pay for the build.

2004 – Funding agreed to establish Intelligent Systems Centre at Magee

2008 – UU reveals plans to build a new £250m campus in Belfast's Cathedral quarter. The university also announces it is buying the lands at Foyle & Londonderry College as part of a 'major expansion' of Magee. After eventually completing the Foyle purchase nine years later, UU 'develops' the land as a carpark. The Belfast campus will ultimately be fully developed at the cost of £400m, necessitating a bailout loan from the NI Executive.

2011 – Ilex's One Plan for Derry, promising to deliver full-time 9400 students at Magee by 2020, is supposedly adopted by the Stormont Executive in its Programme for Government.

2013 – The Derry University Group is established to lobby for an independent university for the North West (NWU).

2015 – UU transfers Psychology and Sociology out of Magee without consultation. In the period from 2008, more than 100 courses – including Hotel & Tourism, International Business, Housing Management, Modern Languages, History, Peace and Conflict Studies, Politics and many IT courses – would be shelved. Up to two-thirds of Arts, Computing & Engineering, Life & Health Science courses offered at the campus are axed or moved away. The One Plan is shelved.

2016 – The demand for a cross-border university in the North West grows, to retain a permanent bridge with Europe after Brexit.

2017 – Incore, widely regarded as Magee's jewel in the crown, is moved to Belfast, sparking outrage in Derry.

2020 – The publication of the two governments' New Decade New Approach agreement guarantees 10000 full-time students at Magee by 2030. Less than a month later, the reconstituted Stormont Executive approves a £126m loan to UU for its Belfast campus, while simultaneously refusing funding for the expansion of Magee.

2020 – The death of Nobel laureate John Hume in August sparks renewed calls for an independent NWU as a legacy to his work.

2021 – The Westminster Levelling Up Committee considers a new university in Derry, and in August, the NI Secretary of State Brandon Lewis publishes a command paper, saying a cross-border university in the North West could play a role in addressing the legacy of the past.

2023 – The Irish government announces €45m funding towards the expansion of Magee.

2024 – The Royal Irish Academy publishes its second report considering how an independent cross-border university would operate in the North West, with Derry as its hub. Identifying chronic regional imbalance in the North, the Academy also recommends the establishment of a higher education oversight committee for NI.